McGRAW-HILL PUBLICATIONS IN PSYCHOLOGY
CLIFFORD T. MORGAN, Consulting Editor

EXPERIMENTS IN SOCIAL PROCESS

A Symposium on Social Psychology

McGraw-Hill Publications in Psychology

CLIFFORD T. MORGAN

CONSULTING EDITOR

EXPERIMENTS IN SOCIAL PROCESS

PROCESS

A Symposium on Social Psychology

Edited by

JAMES GRIER MILLER

*Professor of Psychology, Department of Psychology and
Division of Psychiatry of the Department of Medicine,
and Chairman of the Department of Psychology
University of Chicago*

FIRST EDITION

New York   Toronto   London

McGRAW-HILL BOOK COMPANY, INC.

1950

EXPERIMENTS IN SOCIAL PROCESS

PREFACE

Upon great unsolved questions in the area of interpersonal relations the continuance of our form of civilization depends. Among them are the issues involved in the organization of a stable political and social order for the world that will withstand the pressures leading to war; the problem of dissemination of information to all peoples so that maximum understanding and cooperation will be developed among individuals, groups, and nations; the question of transmission to world leaders of the feelings and attitudes of the great masses, so that governments will be truly representative; and the problem of the development of responsible leaders.

Since such matters are the concern of the social sciences, it is no wonder that these sciences are growing rapidly, both in numbers of persons engaged in them and in money spent upon them. It is also no wonder that social scientists are becoming much more willing to accept responsibility for guidance in effecting social change and forming social attitudes. At the same time there have been development and extension of techniques both for determining accurately the state of affairs in any group at any given time and for changing it predictably.

There is a group of disciplines which might be referred to as the experimental social sciences — or they might be called the sciences of human relations, the sciences of social behavior, the sciences of interpersonal relations, the psychological sciences, or the sciences of man. From the point of view of method, these fields are alike in being more than descriptive, speculative, taxonomic, and enumerative, as are history, classical economics, and certain other areas of the social sciences. They are experimental in the broad sense of the term, that is, they study certain sorts of variability while maintaining other variables constant either actually or by statistical means. They strive toward accurate prediction, achieving it in some instances, and they develop theory on the basis of such confirmation of hypotheses. Isolated studies in psychiatry, economics, anthropology, and political science may meet these criteria, but the majority of the investigations in the social sciences which have employed such methods are psychological or sociological. Psychology has employed precise techniques more extensively than any of the other social disciplines.

The National Roster of Scientific and Specialized Personnel was able to list 28,000 social scientists in 1945. There are, by a recent count, approximately 12,000 journals in the field. Government funds and money from the various foundations have been made available for research to an extent which is not incommensurable with the amount spent on the basic physical sciences.

From all this activity, what is the result? In order to form some idea of the present status of the field of social psychology and to compare and exchange ideas and techniques, a group of social psychologists from various parts of the country were invited to take part in a symposium at the University of Chicago in November, 1947. Representative samples of the most recent work in the field of social psychology were reported and discussed. Investigation of interpersonal relationships is extraordinarily difficult because it requires control of many complex variables. It is possible, however, to design research in such a way that surveys and experiments in the field, researches in the laboratory, and clinical studies may supplement each other to provide insight into human behavior which may be used in understanding the operation of economic forces, the impact of war on individuals, em-

ployee-employer relationships, the functioning of committees, and many similar important practical matters.

It is no accident that throughout the symposium there is a
strong emphasis on methodology. Social psychology has advanced rapidly from the stage of observation and theorizing
to the beginning of experimentation and control, and the
advance has depended upon the development of adequate
tools and the application of careful research design. But the
accent is not wholly on methodology, for we find that
throughout these psychologists are aware of the possible
broad applicability of their results. Group behavior and committee operation (studied both in field and in laboratory
experiments), the question of what makes effective leadership, and the influence upon social activity of an individual's
religion or race are discussed. The value of reliable findings
in this type of research is immediately apparent. The use of
projective material for understanding the motivations and
attitudes of a people is also considered. This is basic research
with definite hope of social application.

The new weapons of mass destruction have dramatized the
fact that the present threat to mankind is of a different order
of magnitude from any other in history. The issues of international cooperation, effective leadership, and accurate social
communication are of unprecedented importance. In the
closing session of the symposium the group of psychologists,
together with a nuclear physicist, turned their attention to
the atomic bomb and similar weapons in an attempt to discover what insight their special knowledge could give into
understanding public attitudes toward it here and abroad,
and to pool their ideas upon what the application of the
findings of social psychology might do to lessen our present
jeopardy.

It is proper that scientists should consider these issues and
face their responsibilities while it is still possible. President

James B. Conant of Harvard has suggested developing a sort of Hippocratic oath for scientists. The tools and knowledge which scientists now have give them so much power that they must be bound by ethical considerations similar to those which physicians have ordained for themselves throughout the ages in order to prevent harm to others. Such an oath should be equally binding upon social and natural scientists, since the forces which both groups are studying and which they can potentially unleash are great and easy to misuse. While it is clearly not within the ability of social psychologists to solve the pressing problems of the day quickly or easily, it can be seen that some of the methods discussed in these papers can be used to make important changes in the desired direction. The research is just beginning, the discipline is young, but we can accurately say that for the first time techniques exist for discovering how people get along with each other, why they fight, and how they can be prevented from fighting. It is a study of good promise, eminently worth fostering.

JAMES G. MILLER

CHICAGO, ILL.
April, 1950

CONTENTS

Chapter 1

SCIENTIFIC METHODOLOGY IN
HUMAN RELATIONS

Donald G. Marquis

Chairman, Department of Psychology, University of
Michigan

Read Feb. 6, 1948, in the Symposium on Research Fron-
tiers in Human Relations. Published in the *Proceedings,*
American Philosophical Society, 92 (6). Used by permission.

THERE is at present an unusual and rather widespread concern with the social sciences — their present status and more particularly their potentialities. During the past two years this has been the subject of several symposia, of several books, of numerous articles, and of hundreds of speeches. It has been debated on the floor of the Senate, and argued, I venture, in most of the administrative councils of our universities and foundations.

The current interest in the potentialities of social science is based on a recognition that many of the crucial issues of our society today are social issues involving the attitudes and convictions and interactions of people. It is further based on a hope that science might achieve in the social field something of what it has achieved in the physical and biological fields.

I suspect that many people who acknowledge the crucial role of human relations are led to a hopeful consideration of social science because of the magic word "science." Certainly never before has there been such widespread and almost devout recognition of the power of science in the physical and biological fields. But it does not take long for such people to begin to suspect that the social science they are examining is not scientific in the same way. Their doubts, of course, are well founded and realistic. The traditional social sciences have developed as a mixture of common sense, speculative philosophy, historical scholarship, religion, wise advice, and some science. This type of development was inevitable and does not differ significantly from the early stages of any field of practical knowledge such as agriculture or meteorology. Desiring some guide in his immediate problems, man has always accepted whatever knowledge he could find — or invent. Scientific knowledge is only one kind of knowledge, and in the field of human relations, it is not easy to come by.

The precise distinction between science and nonscience is a point that the logicians are still studying, but the broad conceptions are pretty generally recognized in the established fields of physical and biological science. The distinction, however, is not clearly made within social science. I propose to examine the nature of current social science, with particular attention to the methods which are employed to secure new knowledge. Many others have undertaken the same task before me and I shall draw heavily from the results of their work.

The first requirement is that we reach some agreement on the nature of scientific method. Many of the formal logical definitions of science do not seem applicable to social science, and I suspect that this is because the logicians have confined their analysis largely to that most recent and highly developed branch of science — mathematical physics. It will be more useful for our purposes to turn to the earlier stages of science, as Conant has done with such profit in his recent book *On Understanding Science*. We should also examine the less thoroughly developed sciences, such as metallurgy, pharmacology, or plant physiology. We will find much more relevant guides for social science by thus broadening the object of our study.

We are impressed first of all by the range and variety of accepted scientific work. Subject matter imposes no apparent limitation. And methods differ greatly from one field to another. Many features ordinarily thought to characterize scientific method are seen to be less than universal. Experiment, for example, is absent in astronomy; measurement is missing in taxonomic biology; theory is relatively unimportant in chemotherapy. Moreover, many of the sciences are grossly inaccurate and unreliable in their predictions. Petroleum geology, epidemiology, and meteorology, for example, are often wide of the mark; yet they are considered very valuable and receive generous support from society.

What, then, is common to each science? A system of logically interrelated concepts, derived from experiment or observation, from which specific predictions can be derived and verified by further experiment or observation. What I have said does not provide any very concrete guide for the application of scientific method in social science, so I would like to go on to a job analysis of scientific research, examining just what is done in the process of building scientific knowledge. It is possible to distinguish a sequence of six steps which can be identified in any complete research. Not all the steps are necessarily carried through by the same scientist. I will name the six steps briefly and then return to show their relevance to social science.

1. Research necessarily begins with the step of *problem formulation*. Questions arise sometimes from practical situations, sometimes from discrepancies and inconsistencies in the current knowledge. But not all questions can be attacked by the methods of science. Problems of aesthetic worth, of ethical value, and of moral choice cannot be directly settled by the kind of research which verifies or refutes a factual proposition. Engineering science can tell us how to build a skyscraper but does not tell us whether the result is more pleasing than a Greek temple. Medicine can predict the effects of inhaling chloroform, but does not tell us whether it should be used for euthanasia. The long-established sciences have found it necessary to separate the value propositions from the factual propositions and direct their research efforts to the latter. Most of the problems in the field of human relations come to us with a mixture of the value and factual elements, and must first be reformulated for scientific study. Such analysis ordinarily poses few difficulties in phys-

ical and biological science but is a frequent source of confusion in dealing with topics like labor relations, race prejudice, or psychotherapy.

There is another common kind of question which must be reformulated before it can be studied scientifically — a question concerning any single and unique event. The older sciences have long accepted the restriction that they can deal only with the regularities of nature — the events which exist in replication. An individual eclipse can be predicted only by a knowledge of the repeated cycles of movement of the planets; a particular patient's illness can be successfully treated only by diagnosing it as an example of what has been studied in many other patients. Social scientists who wish to study a unique phenomenon, such as the United Nations organization, will have to reformulate their questions in such a way as to provide many instances for observation.

2. After formulation of the problem the second step is *review of knowledge* — of what has been learned or said by others about the topic. The library is the usual source of this material, but personal informants are often utilized. The zoologist may talk with a museum caretaker about the feeding habits of the ickabu, and the anthropologist customarily selects a cooperative member of the primitive society for questioning about the culture.

3. The third step is firsthand *preliminary observation* of the events under study. The botanist draws the leaf shape; the clinical psychologist interviews the client; the political scientist attends a meeting of the Interstate Commerce Commission. Such observational work helps to clarify concepts and categories and to suggest methods for measuring them.

4. The fourth step is *theory construction*. Utilizing the concepts that have been developed from previous work and from preliminary observation, the scientist formulates a set of specific hypotheses. Scientists are not the only persons, of course, who make theoretical statements. While the phi-

losopher or the politican may be inclined to believe that his hypothesis is the solution to the problem, the scientist suspends judgment until the appropriate tests have been carried out.

5. The fifth step is therefore *verification* — performing the experiments and observations necessary to support or refute the hypotheses. Highly technical methods are often required to control the conditions and to make the measurements. And since a single observation often leaves the possibility that the result is due to chance factors, statistical methods have been devised for the analysis of multiple data. The test of the hypothesis may be experimental, involving deliberate controlled change of one variable, or it may take advantage of a naturally occurring change or difference in the variable. The test must be carried out on a representative sample of the population to which the hypothesis refers. If the tests do not all turn out as the theory predicted, and this is usually the case, the scientist undertakes to reformulate his concepts to take account of the unexpected results, and then proceeds with further tests of his revised theory. In this manner, theory construction goes along with experiment and observation in a sort of continuous alternation.

6. The sixth and last step in this sequence is *application* of the verified theory. Application involves two further processes: a value judgment or decision to proceed, and a diagnosis to determine that the particular local conditions are appropriate for the theory. Consider the civil engineer building an airport. Scientific theory does not determine whether or not the airport should be built; that decision must be made on the basis of value considerations. The engineer then carries out his diagnosis of local conditions and with his considerable know-how he applies the appropriate knowledge and constructs a particular type of drainage system. The same processes are perhaps clearer in the case of a physician treating a patient. This analysis makes apparent that

those individuals who are charged with the application of science must have two characteristics over and above their scientific knowledge: moral responsibility and diagnostic skill. For this reason a class of professionals is created whose long, careful training will ensure effective application of science.

This completes my job analysis of the steps in the scientific process. A single research project, of course, does not include all the steps, but an effective program of research cannot omit any step. In some of the less thoroughly developed areas of inquiry it sometimes happens that effort is largely restricted to one of the steps. Such projects often pass for science, as indeed they would be if the other steps were added. Let us explore the consequences of exclusive attention to single steps.

Problem formulation often exists by itself in the work of logicians, philosophers, and moralists. A clear-thinking writer may analyze a problem area in order to present the several alternatives, trusting the reader to choose the best. A discussion of criminology may draw the issue in terms of retribution or rehabilitation; an article on perception of distance may contrast Gestalt explanations with behavioristic ones. If any conclusion is drawn it is on the basis of self-evident truth rather than scientific evidence.

Much scholarly work represents a concentration on step 2 — *review of knowledge*. In its most familiar form this is the textbook or handbook. Such publications are very valuable but they are seldom confused with scientific research.

Step 3 — *observation and description* — is more often confused with the total process of research and has been defended as the essential step in science by writers such as Bacon and Karl Pearson. Collection of facts has always been a part of any effective research, but most modern students insist that science includes the formulation of theory based on facts. Examples of sheer fact recording are found in the cataloguing of rocks and minerals, the taxonomic studies of botany and zoology, the collection of census data, and the anthropometry of human skulls. Such facts can be very useful when they are related to a conceptual proposition but by themselves they are not science.

When the fourth step — *theory construction* — is carried out by itself, the result is speculative, philosophical theory rather than scientific theory. Unless the theory is built with concepts derived from the previous step of observation and measurement, it cannot be carried to the next step of verification.

Even the *verification* step can be performed in isolation. Many ingenious experiments are carried out when the hypothesis has not even been formulated, and consequently there is no scientific advance. Twitmyer observed and recorded a conditioned reflex several years before Pavlov, but he did not recognize what he had done. Nature performs many experiments which have no significance to us because we have not asked the question that they could answer. And in the field of social science there is an endless succession of experiments — new laws, new customs, new systems of administration, new economic controls, and so forth. But until the hypothesis is stated, there is no verification or refutation.

The sixth step — *application* — implies by its definition that there is knowledge to be applied. But often it is unverified knowledge and in that case we can speak of application without the support of the other steps in the scientific process. Perhaps legal practice is an example. Without a body of scientifically verified principles, legal advice depends upon a judicious mixture of precedent, common sense, and shrewd estimates of prevailing public sentiment. By way of summary it seems clear that although each of the six steps of scientific procedure may exist alone, it is only by integrated combination of them that we can expect contributions to scientific knowledge.

Let us now turn to look at some of the procedures commonly employed in the social sciences to see how they fit the pattern of scientific method. We shall see that current social science is deficient not so much because it violates any of the steps but rather because it fails to complete the necessary sequence of steps.

Social anthropology has developed a rather distinctive methodology of field observation. Selecting a certain tribe or society for study, the researcher examines the library sources and in addition may interview returned travelers and missionaries. In the field he selects one or more informants for intensive questioning and makes direct observations of the beliefs and activities of the members of the society. He reports his findings accurately, completely, without bias, and in delightfully interesting style, suggesting the interrelations of elements of the culture and the factors producing changes in the culture. It is apparent that he has carried out steps 1 to 3 in commendable fashion. But seldom does he or anyone else carry through to the next step of theory construction. It is true that concepts, such as diffusion, folkways, acculturation, are formulated and defined, but testable hypotheses are not constructed with them. Perhaps this is related to the absence of the right kind of data for testing them. In order to get commensurate data on enough instances to verify a general proposition, it would be necessary for the same researcher to visit many tribes, or to visit a tribe many times over a period of years, or to arrange for other fieldworkers to collect the desired observations in a standardized manner. The cross-culture index at Yale is an attempt to meet this need but it is limited in its use of previous material by the unstandarized manner in which the observations happened to be collected and recorded.

A similar research pattern is seen in community studies in

sociology and in institutional studies in economics and political science such as Thomas and Znanieki, *The Polish Peasant,* Robert Lynd, *Middletown,* and Herbert Simon, *The Administrative Process.* In each case the author records his observations with care and then tries to achieve and communicate an "understanding" or "feeling for" the complex integration. This purpose is well achieved and the studies would be equally valuable as step 3 or in teaching the diagnostic know-how of step 6.

Individual case study represents another pattern of research methodology widely employed in psychiatry, clinical psychology, and social case work. It is similar to the anthropological field method in its emphasis on the unbiased, accurate, and complete description of the object of study. Although serious efforts are directed toward meaningful classifications of individuals and of symptoms and traits, there is little success in formulating generalized principles. Case study, therefore, may be said to emphasize steps 3 and 6 of our job analysis, with less attention to the construction and verification of theoretical propositions. Freudian psychology is of course the outstanding theoretical development. In spite of the fact that Freud formed his concepts on the basis of empirical observation, his theory has been difficult to test because the concepts are not readily identified and measured, and because many of the propositions permit equivocal predictions. The testing of Freudian or other theory depends on our success in devising standardized methods of securing relevant and commensurate data. Recent developments in projective techniques and situation testing offer promise in this direction.

The method of individual case study is also the method of legal study, and recently has been exploited in the new fields of business administration and public administration. It would seem that case-study methods develop when the need for professional application arises before there is a body of tested general concepts or scientific knowledge, and in the absence of a strong academic tradition.

Although case study in its common form does not represent the full pattern of science, it will always have an important place in research method. It is a fruitful source of hypotheses in theory construction; it is essential for diagnosis at the application stage; and it can refute or verify theory if methods are devised for securing commensurate data on different individuals.

Another pattern of research method is found in that phase of *classical economics* which places greatest emphasis on step 4 — the construction of theory. Modeled in part after philosophy, economic theory has been characterized by logical rigor and great generality. The next step of verification has, however, presented unusual difficulties because the concepts are not such as can be directly measured by observation. They were invented on the basis of a priori considerations rather than being abstracted from empirical study. As a result they do not lend themselves to unequivocal test, and it is not unusual to find economists engaged in the dubious practice of reinterpreting their data to preserve their theory unchanged.

Similar types of theory have been propounded in other fields of social science, but none of them has received such extensive development. Examples can be found in Spencer's theory of social evolution, in McDougall's instinct theory, and in Pareto's sociology. A current development is the construction of theory in complicated mathematical form. It remains to be seen whether rational formulations such as von Neumann and Morgenstern's *Theory of Games and Economic Behavior,* and Rashevsky's *Theory of Human Relations* will be capable of empirical testing.

At the other pole of methodology are the *fact-finding* procedures which are best illustrated by the national census. Specifically prescribed by the Constitution of the United

States, the census undertakes periodic collection of data about the individuals, the business and industry, and other aspects of our national life. By the use of statistical techniques, sociologists and economists have been able to distill from these data many significant relationships which permit accurate prediction. Public opinion polls and surveys have greatly extended the possibilities of this type of data collection. Responses are obtained from a carefully selected sample so that the generality of the results is established, and care is taken to secure commensurate data in each instance so that frequencies can be computed and compared. The word "survey" suggests that this procedure is step 3 of our scientific pattern — preliminary observation and description. But closer analysis suggests that the survey is more properly placed in step 5 — the verification process. The concepts to be measured, and their possible interrelationships, are necessarily fixed before the survey can be undertaken. It is not surprising therefore that surveys are not fruitful sources for new hypotheses. Their function is to test existing hypotheses, and the tragedy of many expensive surveys is that so little thought went into the theory underlying the formulation of the hypotheses. In census data we can find, for example, a test of the proposition that more women than men are employed in clerical trades; in a Gallup poll we can test the theory that individuals with high incomes are more likely to vote Republican than Democratic. If surveys are to make their maximal contribution to social science, it will be by greater emphasis on theory construction.

Experimental method is perhaps the most distinguishing method of science and sometimes is identified with science itself. It is, of course, only one of the procedures by which the fifth, or verification, step can be accomplished. Several highly useful and respected fields of science, such as astronomy and geology, are able to make little use of experiment. Among the social sciences there has been quite limited development of experimental manipulation except in psychology where emphasis on method has often been so great as to overshadow the other essential phases of science. A vigorous recent plea for "action research" represents an attempt to utilize the advantages of the experimental procedure without sacrificing the significance of the problems to be studied. By deliberately manipulating the process of social change in real-life conditions and measuring the relevant variables throughout, it may be possible to bring many social phenomena within range of the powerful tool of experimentation.

It is sometimes proposed that the *historical method* is one of the methods of social science. Observations in past time, of course, have the same status in science as observations in the present, and historiography and archeology perform a necessary function in validating such observations. But history is predominantly the selection, synthesis, and interpretation of past events. As such it might seem to be an example of step 3 in the scientific method. Something resembling theory, *e.g.*, economic determinism, is sometimes impressed on the historical chronicle, but such theory does not usually arise out of the historical facts, nor do the facts verify or refute the theory. It may be more defensible to consider history as step 6 — the application of known theory to the events of the past. The practicing physician secures facts about the patient and proceeds to relate and explain them in terms of established medical theory. He will, of course, record different facts and interpret them differently when the theory is changed. So the historian studies the records of the past and applies current social science knowledge to their organization and interpretation. If this process is not very clear at present, it is because social science knowledge itself is not very clear. When verified theory is available it is immediately incorporated into historical understanding.

If this conception of history is correct there would be no expectation that it should contribute to the general store of social science knowledge except in the way that medical practice contributes to medical theory. Contact with the data can sometimes suggest new or revised hypotheses, and clear-cut evidence of a single negative instance can refute a hypothesis.

Just as history represents the application of the totality of social science knowledge to the events of the past, so does the newly developing field of *area study* represent similar application to a restricted region or people in contemporary time. It is not distinguished from social anthropology in subject matter or method, but only in the scientific objective. Anthropology seeks to make direct contribution to general knowledge by the construction of theory and the verification of it with intercultural data.

This brief review of some examples of social science methodology reveals that each step of research procedure has received elaborate development in at least one field. Philosophy excels in the analysis and clear formulation of a problem; librarianship emphasizes the review of previous knowledge; social anthropology and case study provide a model of careful observation and description; economics demonstrates highly developed logical theory; statistics provides excellent guides for verification of theory if the concepts are measurable; and history, business, education, and public administration offer well-organized avenues for application.

The task of social science is thus defined as the coordination of its several specialized skills to produce the complete pattern of procedure necessary for scientific knowledge. The directions of desirable modification are clear. Anthropology and the clinical sciences need more effort in the construction of testable theory; economics needs to develop new theories with concepts derived from observed and measured data;

political science needs further effort in the observation and description stage to suggest the most useful concepts for theory; and survey researches need more emphasis on their underlying theoretical formulations. Perhaps some of these objectives can be facilitated by cooperative interdisciplinary work, but eventually the training in each field should include all the steps in the scientific process.

The difficulties in achieving the full pattern of research are great, and definite compromises and limitations must be recognized. In order to secure commensurate data on many instances for verification, it is necessary to give up the ideal of complete description. To get a theory which is testable it is necessary to sacrifice breadth and scope. To do research which is relevant to critical problems it may be necessary to give up some degree of rigor and the security of working in the better established fields. And to achieve the complete pattern of research procedure it is necessary to give up the desire to get a scientific answer tomorrow to problems like labor unrest, divorce, or world organization. But the lesson of physical and biological science is that verified scientific knowledge with predictive power is achieved only by successively better approximations to the complete pattern of research methodology.

Chapter 2

THE STRATEGY OF
SOCIOPSYCHOLOGICAL RESEARCH

Ronald Lippitt

Associate Professor of Psychology and Sociology, Research
Center for Group Dynamics, University of Michigan

I

THE spectacular unfolding of the results of research in the physical sciences continues to create new and more complex problems of psychological and social adjustment and responsibility. All of us, lay and scientist citizens alike, are posing the crucial questions: Can we achieve a basic scientific understanding of present behavior, and of the potentialities for new modes of behavior, on the part of small and large groups of men living and working together? And can we translate such basic understandings into new, practical realities of creative mastery and development of ourselves and our environment?

In taking this brief look at several problems and forms of current research methodology in social psychology it is relevant to cast a glance at the recent past, for perspective. This gives us a rather heartening picture of growth continuing at an accelerated rate.

Historically, social psychologists have ventured very timidly and ineffectively into the analysis of the complex problems characteristic of everyday living. But during the last decade or two there has been a great increase in the number of important social problems which have been approached diagnostically by sociopsychological research methods. Group morale — as a characteristic of the national group (e.g., strategic bombing surveys of Germany and Japan) or of the small face-to-face social unit (e.g., studies of Scout troops) — has become a phenomenon for systematic quantitative measurement. Several new research organizations are now focusing exclusively on the social psychology of intergroup conflict, the minority group position, and scapegoat agressions. The leadership role in the democratic and authoritarian group process has for the first time been put under the searchlight of experimental study. The place of psychological motivations in economic behavior has been revealed by quantitative methods. Systematic experiments have been made on the resistance to change, and the techniques of producing change, in such culture-bound behaviors as what foods families in certain ethnic and economic groups do and do not eat. Pioneering studies have started streams of basic research on the voting behavior of the American citizen, the resistance to rehabilitation of delinquent gangs, the social psychology of convalescence, the reeducation of administrators and other social leaders, the dynamics of social communication via the radio, movie, and newspaper, and the bases of productivity in the industrial work group, the committee, and the professional conference. These are just a few samples of research programs which have begun to apply the controls and quantitative tools of science during the past few years.

Along with this trend of focusing scientific energy on a wider range of socially crucial problems has gone a second trend, the creation and refinement of more powerful scientific tools and methods, more capable of exploring systematically the basic properties of sociopsychological phenomena. Much progress has been made toward reliable and fruitful observation techniques for measuring the meaning of the flow of social interaction; the advances in sound-recording techniques, the Lazarsfeld-Stanton Program Analyzer, one-way vision glass, and the development of machine analysis of data have opened up many new opportunities for microscopic quantitative analysis of social behavior; the research on the interview technique has refined a powerful method for collecting quantifiable data on attitude patterns and social motivations; progress has been made on the procedures of content analysis to get at the explicit and implicit values and ideologies communicated through mass mediums; and a number of sociometric devices have been created for measuring efficiently the structure of interpersonal relations that exist in a given group. Many of the so-called "intangibles" of individual and group psychology are becoming concrete and measurable as this tool development continues.

A third trend, perhaps most important of all, is that in the last decade we have been learning to apply experimental methodology to the study of a great range of group behavior. The first carefully controlled experiments on complex group phenomena took place only a decade ago. The possibilities and fruitfulness of such experimentation will be evident in the papers of Festinger[1] and French[2] later in this symposium. The application of experimental manipulation to special characteristics of larger and larger social settings has become a very exciting horizon as we have begun to explore it.

The fourth trend is less developed but clearly evident. Only during the last few years have theoretical structures for the systematic interpretation of social phenomena begun to cut across traditional academic disciplines. Not only do we find theory providing more direction in the formulating of hypotheses for next research steps in social psychology today, but concepts which have been developed in anthropology or sociology or economics or individual psychology are all beginning to have a place in the theorizing on a given problem. During the past year the international journal, *Human Relations*, has been established to stimulate such steps toward the integration of the social sciences.

These four trends (more important problems, improved techniques of measurement, application of the experimental method, and development of theory) have been paralleled by and in many ways are dependent on another development of the war years — the discovery on the part of many social leaders that the social psychologist, along with other social scientists, is needed as a consultant in many areas of prac-

[1] See Chap. 3.
[2] See Chap. 6.

tical judgment and action. This development has resulted in the opening up for scientific analysis of many hitherto inaccessible segments of society. The demand for such analysis is growing more rapidly than is the supply of new social psychologists to fill this need.

This type of backward glance is likely to give today's social psychologist a glow of optimism when he sees the acceleration of scientific growth that is in evidence. But this is very quickly dispelled by a realistic look at the minute amount of our total national scientific energy and resources that is being devoted to basic research in this field, and the lateness of the time.

II

With this sketchy perspective let us turn now to an examination of some aspects of the developing strategy of sociopsychological research methodology as we see them in our current research operations, particularly in reference to (1) problems of research control, manipulation, and measurement, and (2) the relationship between sociopsychological research and social change.

Research Controls

The experience of other sciences where experimentation is possible reveals that when experimental methodology becomes preeminent as the means of exploration and analysis, a great spurt is made in systematic understanding and empirical richness. The growth of our insights in social psychology as the result of recent laboratory experiments on group panic; on democratic, authoritarian, and laissez-faire leadership; on group frustration; on the operation of prejudice in voting, etc., lead us to the conviction that this same spurt will take place in the development of a systematic social psychology of group behavior.

Of course some of the psychological phenomena of the social universe are still as untouchable as the stars when it comes to applying directly experimental manipulations and controls. We are not able at the moment, for example, to set up experiments on United Nations committee behavior in order to study some of the variables relevant to the course of international relations. But let us take a look at our battery of research methods as we might use them to get basic understandings which would be applicable to the international committee situation. Just as an example, let us set up a hypothetical research project which will have the double research objective of (1) getting some basic understandings of committee operation that will be applicable to the international committee, and (2) getting some understandings of ways of producing change for the better in such committees. In this illustrative research program we will distinguish between the contributions to be made by four types of research method: (1) the field survey, (2) the field experiment, (3) the laboratory experiment, and (4) the clinical analysis of the single case. Examples of these methods will be described in greater detail by other contributors to this symposium.

First, we would like in our hypothetical project to obtain a good diagnostic understanding of what kinds of problems come up in committee operation, whether they are quite different or similar for various kinds of committees, what the experience of committee members is in committees with various purposes. We decide to make a *field survey* of a sampling of committee members and leaders, using a comprehensive interview, to get the best over-all perspective and understanding of committee life as a starting point. Our sample is drawn in such a way that we get representatives of the universe of committees in our survey sample. In preparing for the survey we do a pilot study of a number of committees which are easily accessible. In the analysis of the data we find that there is a great generality of the incidence of various problems of committee operation as reported by members; but there seems to be one rather significant difference between committees where each member is representing a different group, and committees which are subunits of a larger group of which they regard themselves as a part. In the first type of committee the data suggest a special phenomenon of conflicting loyalty to the member's own group which he represents and loyalty to the committee to which he belongs. From the breakdowns of the quantitative analysis of the interviews we see some very interesting intercorrelations between certain descriptions of committee chairmanship and what seems to happen in such committee meetings. We get only very limited insight, however, into the causes of committee efficiency or inefficiency, or into the ways in which committee operation can be changed. The field situations from which we have drawn our data have varied so greatly in regard to a great many factors over which we have had no research control that no clear-cut generalization about causation can be made. We do have a wide variety of hypotheses we would like to test out: for example, the effect of getting certain types of agreement as to committee goals.

Second, we feel ready now to set up some *field experiments* where we can study the two major types of committee intensively under more controlled conditions, introducing planned changes to test the various hypotheses concerning the relation between the way the chairman leads the meeting and the productivity of committee operation. Because of the relationships the research unit has built up through previous researches and consultant services, there are several organizations that are asking for help in improving staff meetings and committee process. In return for such services they are ready and expecting to collaborate in any necessary measurement operations. We decide to work with four committees, from among the larger number who are interested in getting help, in one large organization.

Two of the selected committees are made up of members representing competing departments where each member must "bring home the bacon" to his own department. The third and fourth committees are subcommittees of one department. After a brief orientation phase the research is so well accepted that special checks indicate there is no observable effect produced by the microphones on the table and the observers in the room. The questionnaires and interviews are also accepted as a step toward getting some valuable help. After a period of data collection to get an accurate sample of committee life, a member of the research team who is also skilled in the techniques of group education and therapy begins to work with each committee to induce specific changes in committee operation. The research staff do their best to record and track down the interpretation of the various changes that result from these change-experiments. New variables that could not be discovered in the field survey emerge in bold relief. It is discovered, for example, that the behavior of the chairman is strongly determined by his perception of the expectations of the committee members. This shows up as a phenomenon of resistance to changing his behavior in the experiments. In the two committees made up of representatives it is discovered that the type of contributions a given member makes in a meeting are highly related to the way in which he perceives his loyalty to the committee and to the group he represents. When these perceptions are changed by increasing the importance of the committee membership through the training procedure, great changes in committee productivity occur. The experiment teaches us a great many things about what factors are related to each other in making for productive or unproductive committee functioning, and how changes in some of the factors can be produced. No definitive interpretations can be made from this field experiment as to how any one particular variable functions and how it is related specifically to other variables; because a number of factors have been varying at once — there has been no careful matching of groups, and other controls needed in a refined experiment have been lacking. But, as Dr. French's[3] paper will point out, there are immediate practical applications of such action-research, as well as contributions toward more basic fact finding. From the discoveries of this experiment the researchers feel they are in a position to set up some clear-cut, refined postulates about, for example, the ways in which this member-self-perception variable will relate to the subject's behavior in decision making, intermember aggressiveness, and other factors. The research staff also feel fairly secure that they have discovered the relevant variables which they will need to control in order to explore the single factor they want to analyze more fully.

Therefore, it is possible to take a third step in the research program: setting up some *laboratory experiments* in the room they have equipped for group experiments to test the postulated law covering the relationship between the degree of conflicting membership and the nature of contribution to committee functioning. This time each group is made up of strangers, so that the total group history can be controlled. The membership composition of each group is matched for factors which were found to be important in the field experiment. Specific group loyalties are built up around the planned activities in each group, then cross-group activities are begun in which members are each representing their own group, with experimentally varied degrees of pressure to "bring home the bacon" on specific conflict issues. The type of committee chairmanship is varied systematically, and the predictions made before the experiment began are checked by the various observation and interview measurements which are being made. Our data seem to indicate meaningful lawful relationships of the

[3] See Chap. 6.

type predicted between the factors of group membership identification which have been systematically varied and the content of contributions. The field survey showed a wide generality of these variables in many types of committees so that we feel we have a fairly powerful generalization. Also we have a number of findings about the effect of committee chairman behavior on this relationship.

Fourth, what if, by some chance, committee X of the United Nations asks for some consultation? Perhaps the chairman has read the report prepared by a group of social psychologists at the request of the Social and Economic Council proposing a United Nations Institute of the Human Sciences,[4] in which a project on international committee productivity is included. As is true in all sciences, we would have no concrete applications to recommend from our general law without a diagnostic study of this particular committee. We would now be able to make this analysis efficiently, with well-developed instruments. Once we found out what factors were present and to what degree we could make interpretations from our basic data about the variable of conflicting loyalty. Our efficiency and helpfulness in this clinical analysis of the specific case will depend on the comprehensiveness of the theoretical structure we have been able to build up from our basic research explorations, as well as our skills in communicating these data and their implications to the committee in question.

We see from this illustration that a basic research program on group life calls for a balance and integration of research designs, including systematic field surveys and clinical case studies of individuals and groups functioning in their customary way; more controlled field experiments in the real-life setting where planned changes are introduced; and well-controlled laboratory experiments. Any particular research project may require a well-planned se-

[4] Proposal for the establishment of a United Nations Institute of the Human Sciences. *Human Relations*, 1948, I (3): 353–373.

quence of such designs to yield the most fruitful theoretical insights and generalizations for technological application.

Measurement and Theory

The necessity of dealing with more and more complex problems of social behavior has led social psychologists to see that to a much greater extent than in any of the other sciences the human being is a part of the measurement operation. In observations of the stars or the reading of a gauge the personal equation is important but involves a restricted psychological function. In the early work on using human beings as quantitative observers of social behavior all efforts were bent toward minimizing the complexity of the judgments to be made by the observers in recording on a check list the frequency of certain units of behavior. This work resulted in sterile categories of observation, with behaviors of the same physical or grammatical form put in the same frequency category rather than social behaviors having the same meaning but perhaps quite different manifestations. We are finding now that the human observer, or interviewer, or coder of a recording, can be calibrated to do a reliable job of using the highest degree of social sensitivity to which he can be trained.

The recent surge of creative development of measurement techniques in social psychology is to a major extent, I believe, a symptom of another trend I have referred to — the growth of theory construction. When social psychology was almost entirely at the crudely empirical level of grubbing around for facts for the sake of facts, a limited number and type of measurement tools provided adequate apparatus to play around with to see what interesting intercorrelations among social data could be found. This situation has changed as more complex problems demanded more systematic comprehension. The necessary theory building has in turn pointed out crucial blind spots in our empirical knowledge where no adequate measurement tools have been developed. Currently we find such developments in the fields of social perception, the measurement of the relationship between values and behavior, tests of group resistance to change, and others. At the present stage of our science it is exciting to note the increasing number of social psychologists who see that disciplined conceptualization in social psychology is the path to fruitful empirical research, as well as the path toward the more distant integration of the human sciences.

III

Kurt Lewin often stated, and aptly proved on many an occasion, that "there is nothing so practical as a good theory." In line with this sentiment I would like to make a few concluding observations on the relationship between social change and the strategy of sociopsychological research and theorizing. First of all, we are discovering that the application of the experimental method in social psychology brings us face to face with the practical technique problems of social therapy and social change. To bring about planned changes in committee operation or the way of life in a housing project requires that we must as scientists master the social skills of producing change. This results in the need to systematize our knowledge about the process of change. Therefore the dynamics of change in group life has become a focal point of our research program, just as the therapeutic process in helping individuals change has become an important focal point in individual psychological research. This type of basic research emphasis brings us into direct communication with the applied sciences of education, group work, group therapy, industrial relations, social work, etc. These professional practitioners have been justifiably pessimistic in the past about the negligible help they could expect from sociopsychological research as it seemed to be developing. For example, the great mass of data on prejudiced and distorted attitudes or on the phenomenon of delinquency supplied very little data to the practitioner on how to approach scientifically the job of doing something about these attitudes or these pathological group behaviors, very little about the dynamics of resistance to and acceptance of changed attitudes, or group codes. As a result the social practitioner has been forced to depend on the slow, inefficient, and often misleading accumulation of experience, while the physical technologist, with his close communication to meaningful basic physical research, has moved ahead by leaps and bounds. I believe this situation is now being changed with the new research trends in social psychology. Systematic theory is being built and empirical data are being collected which are directly relevant to such crucial applied questions as how groups can be taught to analyze and solve their own problems of inefficiency; how the citizen will react to a contemplated change in a program of government service; how leaders can be trained in the complex skills of social leadership; what types of social organization will facilitate the type of communication needed for optimum living and working relations; what can be done therapeutically about such group pathologies as nonparticipation of members, decision difficulty, subgroup charge.

As leaders and groups learn to use the help of social psychologists in releasing and controlling social energy, the opportunities and resources for fruitful research are beginning to multiply beyond our expectations and beyond our current abilities and man power. The many new opportunities for applied research will throw the strategy of research out of balance unless the opportunities for basic laboratory experimentation and theory refinement are also provided on a much larger scale. Only by proceeding on such a coordinated methodological front, with the types of research teams which are implied, can social psychology make the contributions of which it is potentially capable at the rate they must be made.

Chapter 3

LABORATORY EXPERIMENTS:
THE ROLE OF GROUP BELONGINGNESS

Leon Festinger
Assistant Professor of Psychology, Research Center
for Group Dynamics, University of Michigan

IN recent years the field of social psychology has advanced sufficiently so that it is now possible to do strictly controlled laboratory experiments in many areas. What is important is that it is now possible to do these experiments so that they effectively add to our understanding of the dynamics of the behavior of groups in real-life situations.

The social psychologist who attempts to do such experimentation, however, is faced with a number of difficult decisions which he must make. He must ask, first: do I know enough about the area I am investigating so that I may be confident that I will be dealing with important factors? second, do I know enough about these important factors so that I can adequately measure, control, and manipulate them in the laboratory? and third, is my theoretical understanding sufficiently well advanced so that I can state specific hypotheses in a form amenable to precise scientific answer?

Thinking through the answers to these questions on a specific problem makes it clear that before we can begin to use the powerful technique of laboratory experimentation effectively, we must already have gained much understanding by means of other techniques, such as observation of uncontrolled situations and field experiments under less strictly controlled conditions.

But laboratory experiments alone will not be sufficient, no matter what the state of development of social psychology may be — now or in the future. Without the constant checking against field situations and without the continual supplying of ideas from the field to the laboratory, the laboratory investigator runs the risk of having his research become fruitless, sterile, and unimportant.

Without the rigorous and precise explorations of the laboratory, the field investigator risks the danger of building up an insecure structure with tentative hypotheses resting on inconclusive results.

The science of social psychology must indeed progress by means of an integration of various methodologies.

The controlled laboratory experiment is *not* an attempt to duplicate, in miniature, a real-life situation. It is rather an attempt to set up the pure case. In other words, it is an attempt to take a factor or cluster of factors which we have good reason to believe are important and systematically vary them in a context where other factors are well controlled. By such means we may begin to build up a body of knowledge concerning the precise functional relationships between these factors and the behavior of human beings in social situations.

The laboratory experiment can give us the empirical laws of behavior. It does not immediately tell us how to apply these laws to the real-life situation. To permit application we must proceed to the diagnosis and measurement of factors which operate in real-life situations, and to the determination of which laws do and do not apply. We must, however, know the laws before we can apply them.

Laboratory experimentation has already made significant contributions in several areas of social psychology. The already famous experiment by Lewin, Lippitt, and White [1] on the effect of autocratic and democratic patterns of leader behavior on boys in recreation groups has had great impact on many applied fields.

Groups of boys were organized into clubs that met one afternoon a week with the experimenter as leader of the group. The behavior of the leader was prearranged so that with some groups he behaved autocratically — he gave orders, he made all the decisions, he planned the activities; while with other groups he behaved democratically — he helped the boys make decisions, he planned the activities

[1] Lewin, K., Lippitt, R., and White, R. K. Patterns of aggressive behavior in experimentally created "social climates." *J. Soc. Psychol.*, 1939, 10:271–299.

together with them, he advised on who did what. The experimental design, of course, was properly counterbalanced so as to equate for such factors as the personality of the leader.

Extensive observation of various aspects of the behavior of the boys revealed marked differences resulting from the two different kinds of leadership patterns. Under the autocratic leadership the boys showed less initiative, more hostile and aggressive behavior towards each other and toward the leader, were less productive. When the leader was absent the democratic groups continued their activities, while the autocratic groups became quite disrupted. The democratic groups made attempts to include all of the members in their activities while the autocratic groups continually used scapegoats as objects of their aggression. These are only samples of the kinds of things which came to light in these studies.

Since then these data have been used to solve such problems as membership turnover in Boy Scout troops, how to train recreation leaders, how to run productive conferences, how to improve educational methods, and others.

Another example of the fruitful approach to a problem by means of laboratory experimentation is the study which was made by French[2] of the reaction of organized and unorganized groups to frustration. In this experiment groups of young people who were already organized for social or athletic purposes were put into an identical laboratory test situation as groups newly formed for this specific purpose. The test situation consisted of working on a problem which required cooperative effort on the part of all the group members for its solution.

Detailed observations of behavior, together with the data collected by means of interviews with members of the groups, revealed marked differences between the organized

[2] French, J. R. P., Jr. Organized and unorganized groups under fear and frustration. *Univ. Ia. Stud. Child Welf.*, 1944, 20:229–308.

and unorganized groups. The organized groups showed more we-feeling and stronger motivation to solve the problem than did the unorganized groups. There was greater equality of participation among the members of the organized groups, while in the unorganized groups some members participated much and others participated very little. The organized groups also showed much more frustration and more aggression when progress toward solution of the problem was blocked.

These findings of the effects of different degrees of organization and cohesiveness on the behavior of groups have had application in tackling such seemingly unrelated problems as those of worker morale and worker productivity in industry. For example, the same factors were found to explain the higher grievance rate among organized work teams than among unorganized individuals. Knowledge of these factors led to finding more successful methods of handling group grievances.

I should like now to give a more detailed description of the procedure and results of an experiment [3] which I conducted to determine some of the conditions under which the behavior and attitudes of people toward other people are determined by the group membership labels of the people concerned. More specifically, the study dealt with a systematic investigation of the effect which knowledge of religious affiliation had in determining one's behavior toward other people.

I shall not try to report all there is to tell about the procedure and techniques used in conducting this experimental study. I shall only attempt to review the more salient features of the design as a necessary prelude to considering the results which we found.

The major theme was to gather a group of people in our

[3] Festinger, L. The role of group belongingness in a voting situation. *Human Relations*, 1947, 154–180.

laboratory who would function as a meeting of a club to elect officers for the club. It was further desired, for the purposes of the experiment, to have the membership of the "club" evenly divided as to Jewish and Catholic religious affiliation.

From the point of view of control over the factors which influence the situation and consequent ability to interpret our results unequivocally, there were a number of major problems which had to be solved.

How could we equate or control the previous history of interactions among the individuals concerned? In any existing group or real-life situation this history, through the attitudes which have developed in consequence of it, has an important bearing on behavior. For the purpose of not allowing this factor to obscure the variable which we wanted to observe in operation, we set up our group meetings so that the people involved were complete strangers to one another at the beginning. No one knew anyone else or anything about them — at least no more about them than he could surmise from looking at them.

This, however, only partly solves our problem. There are still, as everyone knows, marked differences among people. There are people we like at first sight, and there are people we do not like at first sight. With this powerful factor operating we would have a very difficult time singling out the effect which knowledge of religious affiliation had on behavior. Two solutions to this problem were devised, both of which were used.

One solution was to have exactly the same people, in exactly the same group, elect a club officer both before and after they knew the religious affiliation of the others. Accordingly, for half of the group meeting everyone referred to everyone else by means of an assigned number and no one knew the name or religion of anyone else in the group. Halfway through the meeting, on a pretext, it became necessary for everyone's name and religion to be written on a blackboard along side of their assigned number. The meeting then proceeded to further elections.

We were thus able to observe, for the same people, in the same group, in the same voting situation, what effect this knowledge of name and religion had on their voting preference.

Not completely satisfied with this control, however, we also decided to insert an even more rigorous one. Each group was composed of ten girls. They were told that each of the girls came from a different college in the Boston area. (This, incidentally, is quite plausible since there are more than enough such colleges to go around.) Actually, six of the girls at each meeting did come each from a different college. The other four girls, however, were paid participants. These same four paid participants were members of each group and were coached as to how to behave. When the time came for identification by name and by religion, two of these four said they were Jewish and the other two said they were Catholic. However, which two said they were Jewish and which two said they were Catholic changed from group to group. We were thus able to compare how many votes the same people received when identified as Jewish and when identified as Catholic.

We have thus succeeded in setting up a situation which it would be impossible to find in everyday life. The sum of these controls and safeguards enabled us, with a high degree of confidence, to single out changes in behavior due only to knowledge of religious affiliation.

Figure 1 shows the per cent of votes given to Jews and to Catholics before and after they were identified by name and religion. In this, and the subsequent figures, the first vertical bar shows the per cent of votes given to Jews by Jews; the second bar shows the per cent of votes given to Catholics by Jews; the third and fourth bars show the per cent of votes given to Jews and Catholics respectively by Catholics.

It is clear from the figure that before anyone was identified as to religion both the Jewish and the Catholic girls in the groups split their votes equally between Jews and Catholics. All the percentages hover about 50 per cent. We may come

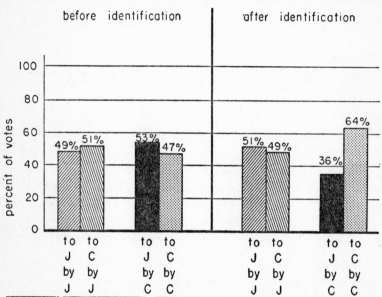

FIG. 1. Per cent of votes for different groups in face-to-face experiment.

to the conclusion, which we certainly would have anticipated beforehand, that among a group as homogeneous as college girls, there is not enough difference among members of different religious groups to outweigh the wide variety of personality factors which make for being chosen an officer of a club.

The effect of knowing the name and religion of the other people introduces a considerable change in behavior. While the Jewish girls still split their votes about evenly between Jews and Catholics, the Catholic girls now give 64 per cent of their votes to Catholics and only 36 per cent to Jews.

Let us examine whether or not this holds up for our more rigorous comparison of votes given to the four paid participants when they identified themselves as Jewish and when they identified themselves as Catholic. The second figure shows these data.

We may see, by examining the figure, that the data are

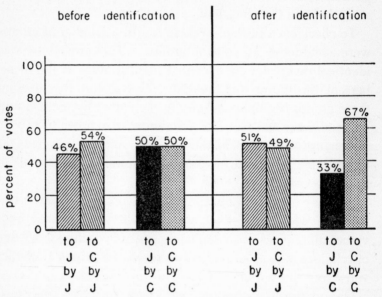

FIG. 2. Per cent of votes for paid participants when identified as *J* or *C*.

virtually identical with the data shown in the previous figure. Before the individuals are identified, both Jews and Catholics split their votes quite evenly between those who later on will be identified as Jewish and those who later will be identified as Catholics. All the percentages are very close to 50 per cent. After the identification is made, the pattern again changes markedly. The Jews still split their votes evenly between those paid participants who identify themselves as Jewish and those who identify themselves as Catholic. The Catholics, on the other hand, give 67 per cent of their votes to those paid participants who identify themselves as Catholics and only 33 per cent to those who identify themselves as Jewish.

It is well to mention once more at this point that the paid participants who identify themselves as Jewish are the same ones who identify themselves as Catholic. Each of the paid participants was identified as Jewish in half the groups and as Catholic in the other half.

To check even further on these results a number of groups were conducted as control groups. The procedure was identical except for the fact that identification of the members of the group was omitted. Throughout the meeting these groups continued to refer to each other by number and did not know the name or religion of the other members. No changes occurred in these groups and the percentages of votes for Jews and for Catholics continued to stay close to 50 per cent.

We may unequivocally come to the conclusion that in this situation where the effect of personality factors and individual differences was adequately controlled, the knowledge of religious affiliation markedly affected for whom Catholics voted, but did not affect for whom Jews voted.

One of the first questions we asked ourselves concerned the nature of the effect of the identification on the Jewish members of the groups. It is possible that they were quite unaffected by the identification. On the other hand, it is possible that the identification may have aroused two sets of conflicting forces, the net result of which was to leave the distribution of votes to Jews and Catholics unchanged.

In an attempt to answer this question, another type of group was set up. In this group 10 girls, half of them Jewish and the other half Catholic (including the four paid participants), sat up on a platform at the front of a large room. About 50 girls sat in the room facing the front platform. The large group of 50 girls did the voting and could vote for any of the 10 girls on the platform. The 10 on the platform did not vote. Halfway through the meeting the 10 girls on the platform were identified by name and religion, as in the previous experiment, *but the girls who were doing the voting were never identified.*

The results for this large group are presented in Fig. 3. The results prior to the identification are identical with the

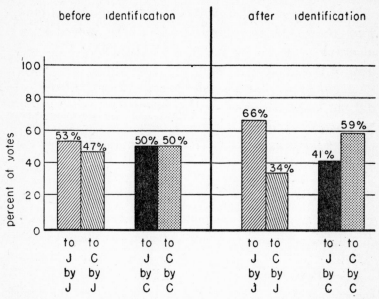

FIG. 3. Per cent of votes for different groups in "large-group" experiment.

results for the small face-to-face groups. The results after the identification, however, present a rather different picture. Here *both* the Jewish and Catholic members of the group have altered their distribution of votes. The Jewish girls give 66 per cent of their votes to Jews and the Catholics give 59 per cent of their votes to Catholics. In short, in the large group the Jewish members of the group are no longer unaffected by the knowledge of name and religion. Indeed they are affected at least as much as the Catholic members of the group.

There must be some real differences between the small-group and the large-group situations to have produced this difference in behavior. Let us recapitulate and interpret these differences.

First, in the small groups the people doing the voting were at the same time the recipients of votes. In the large group the people doing the voting were *not* receiving the votes. It would then seem that in the small-group situation the group members would be concerned with both their reactions to other people and other people's reactions to them. In the large-group situation, however, the voting members of the group would only be concerned with their own reactions to the ten people who were receiving votes.

Second, in the small-group situation all the members were identified by name and religion halfway through the meeting. In the large-group situation only those who were the recipients of votes were identified. The voting members of the group were never themselves identified. In the large-group situation, then, the voting member of the group, whose behavior we are here examining, remained personally anonymous throughout the meeting, while in the small-group situation there was no anonymity for anyone.

It should be emphasized here that this anonymity applies to whether or not anyone knows who the person is and does not apply to knowing how anyone votes. All the ballots in all the experimental situations were secret ballots. All the ballots were, as far as the group members knew, unidentifiable as to who did the voting. They were, of course, identifiable to the experimenter.

How can we understand and explain the results which have been obtained? In the situation where the individual is anonymous and does not have to be concerned with the impression she makes on others, but only with the impression others make on her, we find that both Jews and Catholics react to knowledge of religious affiliation by voting more for members of their own group. We must then maintain that for both Jews and Catholics there are forces operating in the direction of favoring members of their own group. It must also be maintained that this force, for both Jews and Catholics is strong enough at least partially to overcome personal preference for individuals. The reaction to the same individual in the same situation depends on whether or not a religious label is worn and which label it is.

But in the small face-to-face groups the Jewish girls do not show any effect of this identification. We must maintain, then, that in this situation a sufficiently strong counter-force was brought into operation. It is plausible that this counterforce should stem from the factors in the small-group situation which are different from the large-group situation, namely, that the individual doing the voting is not anonymous, and the nature of the situation pushes her to consider the impression she is making on others in the group. It would seem, then, that when the Catholic girl is identified before others as Catholic in a situation where the others are considering whether or not to vote for her, she is still able to express her preference for other Catholics. When the Jewish girl, however, is identified before others as Jewish under these same circumstances, she cannot express her own preferences for members of her own group — perhaps because she fears or feels rejection by the members of the other group.

What are the larger implications of this experiment and the larger implications of experiments such as this that might be done in the future?

Here we have a technique, a means of studying systematically the various facets of phenomena like intergroup conflict, prejudice, and the strength of the influence of group membership. We have already cast some light on the function of secrecy and anonymity in determining people's overt reactions toward others who can be labeled. We have begun to cast some light on the reactions of the members of minority groups to such labeling of themselves, and its effect on their behavior in mixed groups. We have begun to see very specifically what the relative strengths of various factors are in allowing or retarding the overt expression of prejudice.

One small experiment is of course only a bare beginning. Other experiments on these factors can and undoubtedly will follow. The ramifications of the problem are many and the answers such experiments can supply are important. The whole problem of what function group belongingness plays for us and what its effects are, must be the focus of attack by means of such systematic study. What effect does being an American have on our behavior toward other people? What effect does being a Bostonian or a New Yorker have? What effect does being a Southern or Middle Western congressman have?

We have given several examples, one in greater detail than the others, of experiments on social behavior in the laboratory which have furthered our understanding of the dynamics of human behavior. The empirical and theoretical knowledge gained in this manner has enabled us to push faster towards the solution of practical problems with which we are continually confronted.

The development of social psychology has shown the same trend which other empirical sciences have shown. Advances in social psychology have enabled us to bring new problems into the laboratory for close examination and have opened up new areas for study. Today there are still many vital problem areas which we are not able to study systematically. Our knowledge about them is still gained from relatively crude observations of uncontrolled situations.

In the near future, however, we can foresee great strides of progress. Such problems as the effect which social and cultural factors have on the personality development of the child; the nature of group functioning in the life of communities; factors affecting social participation in a democratic society; problems of international relations — in all these areas the beginnings of systematic study by means of field experiment and refined measurement are being made. Soon we will be able to bring these problems into the laboratory.

The difficulties of making rapid progress in social psychology are numerous. At present there are very few laboratories in the country that are adequately equipped to do this kind of research. There are also very few social psychologists in this country who find that they have the time to do such research. The organization of social science research units and research teams which have adequate facilities and abilities will greatly speed this development.

Chapter 4

SURVEY RESEARCH:
PSYCHOLOGICAL ECONOMICS

Dorwin Cartwright

Associate Professor of Psychology and Director, Research
Center for Group Dynamics, University of Michigan

I

WHEN George Gallup successfully predicted the presidential election in 1936, one of social science's most effective tools, the sample survey, was dramatically brought to the attention of the general public. At that time it was a newly fashioned tool, roughhewn and crude, but its essential principles were sound; and it needed only improvement of detail to become an indispensable part of the social scientist's research equipment.

Survey research is based upon two rather simple notions. First, it is assumed that by talking to an individual and by asking the proper sort of questions one can learn much about his past behavior, his current state of affairs, his plans and intentions for the future, his goals, values, attitudes, information — in short, a vast portion of the determinants of his past, present, and future behavior. This may be called the assumption of the *validity of the personal interview*. In making this assumption it is not implied that valid interviews are easily conducted or that unskilled technicians can successfully design or execute them. The assumption merely asserts that such information *can* be elicited under proper conditions of interviewing.

The second notion inherent in all survey research is the proposition that highly accurate estimates can be derived from information about a relatively small sample of a total population. This may be called the assumption of the *validity of small samples*. This assumption, like the first one, asserts merely the possibility of obtaining correct estimates of large populations from properly designed small samples; it makes no claim that all small samples will be accurate.

Taken together, these two notions describe the essential nature of survey research. They assert that by interviewing a small sample of the population it is possible to learn about the behavior, motives, information, attitudes, and intentions of the entire population. It should be clear that if these assumptions can be sustained in actual practice, survey research is indeed a powerful tool. If it can accomplish all that is claimed, it is able to provide social scientists as well as social practitioners with extremely valuable information.

But are the assumptions justified by the facts? Consider the assumption of the validity of the personal interview. Has not Freudian psychology proved that people rationalize, that is, misrepresent their true motives? Is it not our everyday experience that people exaggerate, distort, conceal, or even lie to protect their status or to inflate their ego? These points must in large part be granted, and yet the available evidence tends strongly to support the assumption under question. How did Freud discover that people rationalize? By means of a very elaborate and intensive interview. To my knowledge no one has seriously proposed conducting psychoanalytic interviews with a representative sample of the population to probe the depths of the American psyche, but the fact remains that properly conducted interviews of manageable length have succeeded in revealing a wealth of valid information about behavior and its determinants. We do not yet know where the effective limits of the personal interview lie, but we are certain that they are far beyond our expectations of even five years ago.

How about the assumption of the validity of small samples? Here a more unequivocal answer can be given. Within the past decade statisticians have solved the major theoretical and practical problems of sampling. It is now possible to predict quite accurately the range of error that will result from a sample of a given size selected in a given way. In other words, anyone planning a sample survey can know in advance the approximate precision a given sample will possess before he undertakes his survey. It may be added that although precise samples of the entire population are still relatively expensive to obtain, the size of such samples can be remarkably small.

The quantitative validation of these assumptions is not easy to carry out, and the evidence now available has been gathered largely as a by-product of ongoing research designed to solve practical problems. But even though no single validating test can be considered conclusive, the total body of available evidence tells an impressive story. Let us look at a few examples.

First, estimating national economic data. Survey research conducted for numerous governmental agencies during and since the war has provided ample opportunity for checking survey estimates of various kinds of data against known national totals. For example, following each war loan drive a representative sample of people was asked to report such information as the value of bonds they had bought during the drive, their total bond ownership, or the amount they had redeemed during a given period of time. For all these estimates, of course, actual records of national totals were available. Fairly typical results of such checks of surveys against known totals were those obtained in the survey after the Fifth War Loan. In this survey each respondent was asked to report the number of people in his family owning bonds and the total amount purchased during the drive. Multiplying these reported figures by the sampling ratio, estimates of national totals are obtained. In this way it was estimated that the number of bond owners living in the country was 77,200,000, compared to actual records for total bond owners of 81,000,000. Accounting for the slight difference of definition of universe studied, the relative error was less than 3 per cent. The survey estimate of E bonds purchased during the drive was $3,009,000,000, compared to actual figures of $3,036,000,000. In passing, it might be noted that estimates of national income by surveys have proved more difficult, but that errors of less than 10 per cent have been consistently recorded.

Second, prediction of use by veterans of GI educational provisions. Two or three years before the end of the war a questionnaire (in this case, not strictly a personal interview) was constructed by the Research Branch of the Information and Education Division of the War Department and given to a representative cross section of soldiers to determine how many would like to get more education after the war. Analysis of these data led to an estimate that 7 per cent would go back to full-time school, given a moderate subsidy. In drawing up legislation, this figure was used by the President and Congress in estimating its cost. The educational subsidy finally adopted was somewhat higher than that employed in estimating the number who would make use of it, and it is interesting to discover that postwar statistics of full-time school attendance by veterans show attendance to be about 2 or 3 per cent higher than the original predictions.

Third, predictions of public reactions to government programs. A much more demanding requirement of survey research is that it be able to specify the type of administrative action required to produce favorable reactions from the public. In such matters, of course, exact validating measures are especially difficult to obtain. An example of this sort arose from a study conducted for the Treasury Department late in 1942 just before the establishment of the victory tax. This new tax was the first payroll deduction tax and officials feared that its introduction would greatly reduce the purchase of war bonds through the payroll deduction plan. Investigation of this problem by survey research indicated that these fears were ungrounded provided the tax was introduced to employees in a certain way. The Treasury adopted the suggested plan of introduction and, following the establishment of the victory tax, they were unable to detect any effect of the tax on the payroll deduction of bonds.

Fourth, predictions where distortions in reporting might be expected. In the past few years sample surveys have been conducted to investigate topics which at first glance would seem by their very nature to guarantee failure. The social pressure against redeeming war bonds during the war, many thought, would lead people who had cashed bonds to deny it to an interviewer coming to their door. First attempts to estimate the number of people who had cashed bonds during a given period revealed that from 10 to 15 per cent of those who had redeemed denied it to the interviewer. Improved techniques later in the war reduced this effect to less than 5 per cent.

Perhaps an even more dramatic example of prediction in the face of great difficulties, however, was the estimation of membership of the National Socialist German Workers' Party (the original Nazi organization) from a survey conducted by the United States Strategic Bombing Survey in Germany immediately after the war. From interviews with a cross section of the adult population within the American, British, and French zones, it was possible to estimate total membership in this Nazi organization. Though the true membership figures are not precisely known, several independent estimates are available, including those derived from an analysis of the party's files found in Munich after the war. These various estimates are remarkably similar and indicate a high probability that total civilian membership in this party approximated six million. The figure obtained from the sample survey was 5,646,000. These figures strongly support the conclusion that the interview techniques employed resulted in a remarkably small number of concealments of membership and conflict with the impressions conveyed by many news reports that all Nazis now denied their earlier affiliations.

From these examples the conclusion seems warranted, as a basis for further work, that survey research provides techniques capable of revealing with considerable accuracy important features of human behavior and its determinants.[1] Let us now turn to an examination of a relatively new development in the use of survey research, the study of economic behavior.

II

The economic pressures set up in this country by the sudden conversion from peace to war after Pearl Harbor created problems in social management unparalleled in history. Agencies like the Office of Price Administration, the War Production Board, the War Food Administration, the Treasury Department, and the Federal Reserve Board assumed responsibility for organizing the economy to accomplish two goals: maximal war production and maximal economic stability. Very quickly and very dramatically it became apparent that this task could in large part be stated as a problem in getting people to behave in certain ways. Almost immediately officials in these agencies were heard talking about "incentives," "compliance," "public cooperation," "hardship," "the effect of increased income on the propensity to spend," and a host of other matters not easily classified as

[1] In discussing the validity of survey methods, reference should be made to the failure of the polls in predicting the presidential election of 1948. The reasons for the failure are a subject of controversy, but the following points should be made: (1) Although the winner was consistently missed, the average percentage error of prediction was not as great as in the case of some "successful" predictions. (2) None of the national polling organizations employed the more costly methods of probability sampling which have been developed in recent years and which provided the basis for the predictions enumerated above. (3) There is evidence that a shift in opinion took place among segments of the population between the final poll and the election. Though adequate survey research should be able to predict such shifts to some extent, it is likely that the polls described more accurately the state of opinion a few weeks before the election than the actual voting on election day.

the subject matter of single disciplines in the social sciences. Where should one turn, for example, for guidance in the controversy over compulsory vs. voluntary methods of increasing consumer savings? The matter was clearly the concern of the economist, and yet the crucial issue involved not only political philosophy but whether or not people were so constructed that they would increase their savings adequately as a result of appeals and requests.

The outcome of this situation was that social scientists of many different disciplines found their skills required by these agencies and that new research procedures were developed to provide new types of information. The application of survey research techniques to the area of problems jointly involving economics and psychology is but one of the scientific saltations arising from the nation's hour of crisis. It is a new development, however, which promises to have profound effects not only upon the nation's techniques for handling economic problems but also upon the professional relations between economics and psychology.

An example of some of the developments in this field may be drawn from the work of the Division of Program Surveys of the Bureau of Agricultural Economics. From the beginning of the war this agency conducted survey research for the Treasury Department to aid in guiding policy and action related to problems of inflation control. During a period of more than four years a thorough study was made of the determinants of human behavior as it affected inflationary trends. To illustrate the types of problems investigated and the procedures employed let us examine the research conducted in response to the Treasury's request at the end of 1945 for information permitting a prediction of the course of war bond redemptions during the following year. The end of the war in August had resulted in a marked increase in redemptions and Treasury officials now wanted to know what effects on redemptions there would be as a result of reconversion and the appearance of consumer goods on the market.

Here was a challenge. To the extent that social science is a science it should be able to make successful predictions. But, surely, the reputation of social scientists as predictors of the future has not been a particularly enviable one. Could we have any hope of doing better than average? Could we make predictions with even a moderate degree of confidence? We thought we could. Many factors, we thought, had contributed to the difficulties experienced in predicting economic trends, but one of the most important seemed to be the absence of direct empirical evidence concerning the operation of the causal determinants of economic trends. The technique of prediction most commonly employed was that of extrapolation of curves. Some of these extrapolations were very complicated, taking into account the intercorrelations of variables, but rarely did the traditional procedure of prediction involve any detailed direct empirical analysis of causal determinants.

One important reason for this fact was the absence of any but aggregate data from large populations. Predictions had to be made from such indexes as the number of people employed, total national income, the proportion of national income saved, the amount of money invested in capital improvement, or total inventories in certain types of businesses. Such indexes shed no light on the differential effect that these factors have on different segments of the population; nor do they make provision for differential motivation among different segments of the population. The use of the same indexes by different people resulted in predictions of bond redemptions so widely different as to be of no practical use to the Treasury.

In our attempt to predict war bond redemptions for 1946, then, three steps were taken in the analysis:

First, an analysis was made of the distribution of the total holding of war bonds among the population. By getting information from the same people in our sample about the size of their bond holding, the amount and type of other savings held, the number of people in the family working, the occupations and industries in which they were employed, the family's vulnerability to economic hardship through unemployment, children's sickness, and the like, it was possible to make a number of extremely important statements about those people who, among themselves, owned the bulk of the bonds.

Second, an analysis was undertaken of the determinants of the behavior of people owning various amounts of bonds. Thus, each person from whom all the objective economic data were obtained was also asked questions designed to reveal his intentions and attitudes as they might affect his decision to cash or hold his bonds. For example, we sought to determine whether he viewed his bonds as savings to be spent for the purchase of consumer goods or, as one respondent put it, as a "nest egg to fall back on"; what plans, if any, he had for the use of his bonds and how firmly he held these plans; whether he felt he needed or wanted to make major purchases of consumer goods and how he would plan to finance them; whether he had found occasion to cash bonds in the past. In short, we attempted to discover as much as possible about his view of his bonds, his intentions for their use, the competing demands for the use of his bonds, and to relate all these to the objective analysis of his financial situation and of how much influence his decisions could have upon the total course of redemptions for the nation.

The third step of the analysis consisted of taking the findings obtained from these first two steps and checking the consequences on bond redemptions that might be anticipated from various possible economic developments. Thus, after knowing what kinds of people held the bulk of the bonds and after knowing what kinds of influences might affect them in what ways, it was possible to estimate rather closely the effect upon bond redemptions that would be produced by the appearance of a certain amount of consumer goods on the market or by a certain magnitude of reconversion unemployment.

In principle, then, the prediction of bond redemptions resulted from a threefold analysis of the distribution of bond ownership among various segments of the population, of the determinants of behavior of people owning various amounts, and of the significance of these findings for predicting redemptions under specified broad economic conditions. Let us now examine some of the data obtained in the survey and the predictions made from them. Time will not permit here a full presentation of all the data which were employed in the analysis.

First, what did we discover about the distribution of bond ownership? Confining our discussion to Series E bonds, the findings were, in a sense, paradoxical. While it was true that at the end of 1945 E bonds were widely distributed in the population — roughly three-quarters of the economic units of the country owning some — the great bulk of the bonds were, nevertheless, in the hands of a relatively small group of investors. One way of looking at the degree of concentration is to divide bond owners into groups according to the size of their bond holding. In Fig. 4 three groups have been distinguished: large holders, owning bonds with a maturity value of $2,000 or more; medium holders, owning $750 to $2,000; and small holders, owning less than $750. The figure shows that more than half of the bonds outstanding ($17.7 billion) were held by the approximately six million economic units who owned $2,000 or more, while about one-sixth of the bonds were owned by the more than 21 million owners with holdings of less than $750. Clearly, for predicting bond redemptions it would be unsafe to assume that all owners should be considered equally important.

Several considerations made it appear most probable that this great concentration of bonds would tend to minimize the likelihood that any large portion of the bonds would be used in the year 1946 to meet expenses during reconversion unemployment or to purchase consumer goods. First of all, the occupations of the large holders tended to be those least likely to be affected by reconversion unemployment. Second, the incomes of these large holders were such that they would be better able to rely upon current income or install-

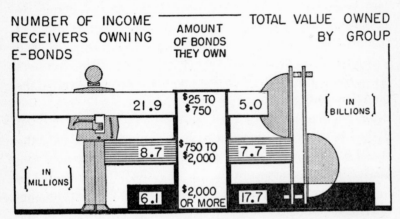

FIG. 4.

ment buying to finance the purchase of consumer goods. Third, persons with large holdings of war bonds were also more likely to have holdings in other forms of saving, thus decreasing the probability that they would use any large portion of their war bonds. Finally, the plans people had for the use of their bonds suggested that there would be great reluctance to cash them for the purchase of consumer goods. Analysis of the interviews revealed that only 5 per cent of all bond owners reported plans to use *any* of their bonds at any time to buy consumer goods. Even if it were assumed that all these people would use all their bonds during the one year for this purpose, their aggregate redemptions could amount to only one and one-half billion dollars, or less than a third of the total redemptions for the year 1945. Further evidence that an immediate buying spree would not bring redemptions in great numbers was provided by the attitude held by most people that 1946 would be a poor time to buy consumer goods because of poor quality and high prices. Although one could not be certain that this attitude would remain unshaken when goods were actually on the market, it did reveal the mood of caution with which the public was approaching the future and, coupled with the reluctance to use bonds to finance such purchases, it reduced the probability that the return of consumer goods would create large-scale redemptions.

Another line of evidence concerning the probable rate of bond redemptions in 1946 derived from answers to a direct question asking each owner when he thought he would redeem his bonds. Only 5 per cent had plans which they expected to carry out during the year 1946, and only an additional 6 per cent thought they would use their bonds before 1951. If it were assumed that those expecting to cash bonds in 1946 were to cash all they owned, they could account for only $1.6 billion, or roughly one-third of the total redemptions in 1945.

Evidence from previous studies of bond redemptions had shown that the major cause for redeeming during the war was the sudden need for cash resulting from some financial emergency. The data collected in this study suggested that the situation would remain essentially the same after the war. When people were asked if they could think of any reason why they *might* cash bonds during 1946, personal emergencies were by far most frequently mentioned. And it is significant that those foreseeing the possibility of the need to cash for emergencies came overwhelmingly from the small holders. Confirming this suggestion that those redeeming for emergencies would be people with small holdings was the finding from an analysis of people who had re-

deemed between V-J Day and the end of 1945 that most of
the redeemers during that period had very small holdings.

Taking all the evidence available from this survey, the
following prediction of the course of bond redemptions could
be made. First, the great bulk of the bonds were in the hands
of people who were planning to keep them until maturity

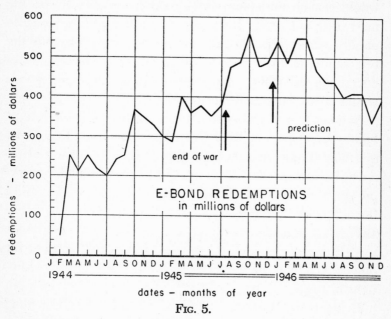

FIG. 5.

and who appeared to be able to carry out their intentions.
The return of consumer goods to the market would increase
redemptions only slightly and the impact on redemptions
would gradually diminish as the small holdings of those
willing to use bonds for this purpose were expended. The
effect of reconversion unemployment or extended strikes
would be to increase bond redemptions slightly, but the
aggregate holdings of people most affected by these events
were not large enough to produce drastic increases, and the
effect of unemployment on redemptions would quickly decline as the small holdings of these people became exhausted.

In summary, the evidence indicated only slight increases in bond redemptions during reconversion and a probable decline in redemptions as smaller holdings were exhausted.

Figure 5 shows how well these predictions were borne out by the course of events. It will be noted that redemptions rose immediately after the end of the war, remained high throughout the winter and spring of 1946, and then gradually declined.

In this research no attempt was made to arrive at a precise figure for total redemptions during the year 1946 since the exact rate of redemptions would depend upon such unknown conditions as the prevalence and duration of strikes and the speed of reconversion. Nonetheless, on the basis of the survey results it was clear that redemptions could only under the most extreme assumptions be expected to fall below $4.5 billion for the year or above $6.3 billion. In actuality, $5.4 billion were redeemed during the year.

III

The fact that this particular research project resulted in a reasonably correct prediction and that it proved to be far more accurate than predictions based on other methods is in itself of minor significance. This project was but one of several that have attempted to study directly the determinants of economic behavior as they actually function in concrete situations. The fact that reasonably good predictions have been possible is encouraging, but only the smallest body of knowledge has yet been accumulated. What is significant is that a remarkably good research tool is now at our disposal and that a whole new set of facts can be readily discovered.

Out of the wartime analysis of the determinants of bond buying and bond redeeming has developed an annual survey of consumer spending and saving sponsored by the Federal Reserve Board. Since the end of the war a wealth of data has been accumulated concerning the spending and saving behavior of the American people. If this research is continued over a period of economic change, perhaps throughout a complete business cycle, we shall for the first time have adequate empirical data to test most of the current economic theories concerning the causes of business cycles — at least in so far as the distribution of income, rates of spending and savings, and similar consumer behavior are concerned.

The use of such data in guiding national economic policy has possibilities yet unexplored. Survey data collected in recent years have been used by business and labor leaders in setting policy; they have been cited by the President's board of economic advisors in making recommendations for legislation. To the extent that such research can give a greater time depth to our economic thinking a step will be taken toward more rational action in our efforts to achieve economic stability.

The survey method need not be confined to the study of the economic behavior of individuals as wage earners or consumers. Similar techniques can be applied to study the determinants of decisions of businessmen or even to a study of the determinants of the setting of corporation policy. Though the technical difficulties in such research will for some time be enormous, there is no reason why important data cannot be gathered almost at once.

The full array of possible applications of this technique and of this approach have not yet been explored. Certainly, many of the classical controversies in economics can be settled once empirical studies of this sort become accepted research procedure. The effect of increased or decreased income on the propensity to save, for example, is a matter that can now be observed, and continued speculative controversy may be enjoyable but beside the point. Similarly, the effect of rising wages upon the readiness to invest in the creation of new capital can be studied empirically. Most important, the development of techniques for the study of the determinants of economic behavior will remove from economic theory the need for speculation about the nature of economic man. It will make it possible for psychology and economics to combine their efforts and work together toward a truly empirical science of man as man, be he economic or psychological.

Chapter 5

SURVEY TECHNIQUES IN
THE EVALUATION OF MORALE

Daniel Katz

Program Director, Survey Research Center
University of Michigan

In his research report, Cartwright [1] pointed out some of the achievements and possibilities of the survey method in the field of economic behavior. Now let us continue the discussion of the survey method with reference to the evaluation of morale and related problems. It is important for a number of reasons to recognize that the survey method should be considered in a broader frame than is suggested by opinion polling and election prediction. In the first place, there have been a number of technical advances in the field of survey methods. Interviewing techniques have been developed which go beyond the brief polling interview with its fixed-alternative or yes-no type of question. These methods are similar to the nondirective technique of Dr. Rogers in which respondents are encouraged to tell the story in their own terms so that we know something of the perceptual-cognitive frame of the individual. This intensive, or depth, interview also gives more adequate and valid information about the motivation of the respondent. There has moreover been important progress in the field of sampling so that by and large the problems of sampling are no longer major problems in the conduct of the research. The quota-control method of the opinion polls has been replaced by area sampling. Area sampling gives high precision because it permits no play for interviewer selectivity — the source of the constant bias in the polling procedure toward overrepresenting the upper educational groups. Moreover, the survey method is not limited to materials obtained through the interview. It can take into account objective sources of data already available, such as plant records on productivity or turnover in studies of industrial morale, as well as behavioral observation.

But these technical improvements are of minor importance

[1] See Chap. 4.

compared to the major advance in survey methodology —
the growth of the conception of research design as the basic
frame for the planning and execution of a survey. In other
words, the problem to be studied is regarded from the broad
framework of scientific experimentation. Thus, by research
design we mean the identification and localization of variables at some level of generality beyond the immediate
datum of a given experience, and further, the measurements
of these variables so that we can discover the functional relationships between them. This clearly goes beyond the usual
concept of opinion polling, which emphasizes the reporting
of the incidence of specific opinions in the population.

The difference between the survey method and the experimental approach of the laboratory is that in experimentation
one can manipulate the variables directly, while in surveys
it means getting into real-life situations and taking the variables in the setting in which they occur. Hence problems
must be followed over a period of time, and control obtained through statistical manipulation rather than by direct
action on the variables. The logic, however, is not essentially different from the logic of scientific method in the laboratory. The greatest weakness at the present time is on the
theoretical side — developing the proper conceptual framework for a study so that we evolve principles which tran-
scend a single situation. It is at this point, where theory is
translated into significant research hypotheses, that there is
the greatest need for progress.

One illustration of research design in the survey field can
be found in the study of the effects of strategic bombing
upon German morale. This study was conducted during and
after the war by the Morale Division of the United States
Strategic Bombing Survey under the direction of Dr. Rensis
Likert.[2] There were two popular theories current during the

2 *The effects of strategic bombing on German morale.* Washington,
D.C.: *United States Strategic Bombing Survey, Morale Division,* U.S.
Government Printing Office, May, 1947.

war about the psychological effects of bombing. Some people thought that morale was enhanced by bombing, that what we needed in our own country was a good bombing to arouse us and energize the civilian population. Others held that bombing could demoralize a people so completely that their war effort would falter and that they would finally overthrow their own leaders and sue for peace.

The problem of the psychological impact of bombing thus had both practical and scientific interest, but there were some unusual difficulties in applying a research approach. For one thing, the Germans could not be studied at first hand at the time of the bombing. Their later accounts would be subject to errors of retrospection. When they were interviewed, their situation had already changed either in that their nation had been defeated or that they themselves were no longer subject to bombing. Another difficulty was the nature of the relationship of the German civilian to his conquerors. Would the Germans, consciously or unconsciously, distort their reports of their experiences, their feelings, and their attitudes in talking to American investigators?

Fortunately, it was possible to obtain checks on both these possible sources of error in a number of ways. The retrospective error was minimized in one pilot study by interviewing in two occupied German cities while the war with Germany was still in progress. A more crucial check was possible, however, through a study of captured German civilian mail. A content analysis was made of a large sample of these letters on several dimensions of morale. Since the letters were written at the time of the bombing and since they were not intended for American eyes, they were free of the types of error just referred to. The results of the content analysis could then be compared with the interview findings.

The most important check, however, came from the basic research design of the study. This design postulated, as the major independent variable, the objective facts of the degree of exposure to bombing and provided for their measurement independent of the measurement of morale factors. The dependent variable was the degree of morale and it was measured in terms of its attitudinal and behavioral components. In addition a number of intervening variables which mediated between bombing and morale were studied — for example, the degree of Nazi identification, the effect of other military events, the adequacy of air-raid protection and of postraid relief. In many social science studies it has been difficult to obtain a measure of the major independent variable without involving it with measures of the dependent variable. In this study of German morale, however, the objective measures of bombing were obtained independent of the measures of morale. The British and American air forces had careful records on the tonnage of bombs dropped on every German town. Moreover, as the survey group proceeded through Germany it was possible to make observations of the actual destruction and discover the percentage of homes destroyed in the various towns and in specific neighborhoods within the towns.

The fact that these independent measures of bombing were available made possible the interviewing of German civilians through an indirect approach. It was not necessary to ask them about their experiences in raids or their reactions to bombing. An interviewing schedule was developed for three-fourths of the sample which made no direct reference to bombing until the very end of the schedule. The questions on this schedule were concerned with the usual dimensions of morale: confidence in leadership, war weariness, internal unity, equality of sacrifice, determination to carry on, and so forth. A sample was drawn to reflect the various degrees of bombing exposure from unbombed towns to towns that had been more or less destroyed. Hence it was possible to relate the measures of morale to exposure to bombing and assume, with other factors equated, that the differences in morale corresponding to the bombing differential were not a function of retrospection or German duplicity. Thus even though not all Germans may have responded fully and frankly, the absolute level of candor was not too significant. The study dealt with relativities and not with absolute measures. As a matter of fact, however, rapport was easily established with German civilians immediately after V-E Day. The Germans were glad an end had come at last and were pleased that they were being occupied by the Americans rather than the Russians. The validity of the interviewing material is indicated, moreover, by Helen Peak's analysis of the number of Nazis in Germany, based on the answers to questions in the bombing survey.[3] This estimate of the number of Nazis agreed closely with the estimates made on the basis of captured party files and cards.

The captured German mail, after decoding, was also referred to a category of bombing exposure determined by the bombing experience of the town in which a given letter was written. Two other types of checks were made. One was a study of French *escapees* through the use of detailed interviews. These were Frenchmen held as prisoners in Germany who in the closing months of the war escaped to our lines. Another check consisted of a study of displaced persons — Russians, Poles, and French — who had spent most of the war in Germany.

The results of the whole study can be summarized briefly as follows. Contrary to the notion that under bombing people are energized to greater war effort, the findings definitely showed that bombing lowered German morale. It produced defeatism, war weariness, and apathy. It brought home to the German civilian population, protected in part from the true state of affairs at the front by a tight censorship, a realization that the war was lost. The temporary anger sometimes aroused during the raids was not of much use to

[3] Peak, Helen. Observations on the characteristics and distribution of German Nazis. *Psychol. Monogr.*, 1945, 59 (6):1–44.

the German war effort. It finally tended to be directed more against their leaders than against the Allies who were not convenient targets for the release of aggression.

Although psychological morale was adversely affected by bombing, there was no straight-line relationship between degree of bombing and degree of lowered morale. Relatively light bombing produced almost maximum morale effects. The continuous heavy pounding did not result in continuing and proportionate morale decrements. This is more understandable if a distinction is made between behavioral and psychological morale. Psychological morale refers to the subjective and attitudinal side of the determination to carry on to victory. Behavioral morale is what people actually do about their ideas and beliefs. Indexes of behavioral morale were sought by investigating absenteeism and productivity in German industries and the extent of disruptive and subversive activity in various German communities. The general conclusion was that there was a time lag between lowered psychological morale and its effect on the behavior of German civilians. The German people kept contributing to the war effort until the closing months of the war. Production held up very well during the first nine months of 1944. There was no conclusive evidence of increasing sabotage and subversive activity under heavy bombing. But in the final months of the war came the complete collapse — the consequence in part of an undermined psychological morale.

Another way of describing these results is to say that the dimension of morale can be broken down into two subscales. One scale would have high identification with and high motivation for the war effort at one end of the scale and apathy and indifference at the other. The second scale would start with apathy and would culminate in actual overt resistance to the war regime — definite acts of subversion or sabotage. Increased absenteeism in industry would fall somewhere in the middle of this second scale depending upon its extent and motivation. Now, bombing made the people psychologically depressed about the outcome of the war and created an apathetic state of mind about political matters. People were too concerned about the problems of a foxhole existence, of how to stay alive and keep going from day to day, to be actively interested in anything else. Moreover, in a police state with rigorous controls over the individual, even the apathetic could be kept in line in supporting the war effort. The German people lacked both the will and the means to overthrow or even seriously embarrass their leaders. Thus, while apathy and defeatism were easily produced through air attacks, to give a maximum effect on the first type of morale scale, there was no corresponding shift on the second scale away from apathy and toward an active resistance movement. It should also be mentioned that the German civilians seemed to be suffering from a "little people" complex. From their point of view political decisions were made by high officials and even though they were sick of the war, they as little people could do nothing about it.

It was of interest to find that identification with the Nazi cause, one of the intervening variables postulated, was not in itself strong enough to counteract the depressant effects of bombing. The absolute morale level of the more Nazi-identified civilians was higher before bombing than was the level for less Nazi-identified people, and it was also higher at the end of the bombing. But it suffered just as great a decrement as did the morale level of the non-Nazis. Another variable which it was assumed might mediate between bombing and morale was the psychological preparation of the people for air raids. The original hypothesis was that bombing would be less of a psychological shock to those who had some preliminary mental preparation than to those who had no expectation of being bombed. The facts, however, were in opposition to the hypothesis. The people who expected to be bombed and had thought about it before the raids over Germany became serious, were imaginative and apprehensive individuals who were more adversely affected by bombing than their more stolid countrymen.

The general findings, obtained through interviews with the cross section of the German population, were confirmed by the analysis of captured German mail, by the interviews with French *escapees* and by the study of the displaced Russians and Poles. A minor point of difference concerned the extent of demoralization as a result of bombing. The displaced persons gave accounts of greater demoralization and fear among the Germans than the Germans themselves reported. Though three-fourths of the German sample were interviewed in a schedule which asked no direct questions about their experiences during the raids, the remaining one-fourth were questioned directly about these experiences. The same relationship of an initial heavy morale decrement and diminishing returns with increased bombing appeared in both the direct and indirect approaches. The absolute effects, however, appeared greater in the answers to the direct than to the indirect questions. Probably the direct questioning with its positive suggestion may have overestimated the morale effects of bombing, while the indirect approach may have minimized the effects. Finally, it should be added that a subsequent study of Japanese morale conducted with the same methods revealed the same general pattern of findings.

Another example of the use of the survey method in the study of morale can be found in the investigation of worker morale in American shipyards during the war. Shipyards varied tremendously in their productivity — one yard might take three times as long to turn out the same type of ship as another yard. This was due in part to such technical factors as the flow of materials, the experience and technological know-how of the older yards, and the technical equipment of the company. But it was also due to the motivation or morale of the workers. In the design of the study, we were interested in the relative effect of two sets of independent variables upon the motivation of workers. One set of factors was the out-plant conditions — housing, community living, transportation. During the war, workers who were attracted to the shipyards, as well as to other war industries, had to accept difficult, congested, housing conditions often making family separation necessary, and a hostile community attitude against the interlopers as well as long hours of transportation to and from work. The other independent variable comprised the in-plant factors — the earnings and promotional possibilities on the job, the working and safety conditions within the plant, the treatment by management and supervision. Five yards were chosen for intensive study, an old South-coast yard with bad out-plant living conditions, a new Pacific-coast yard with similar undesirable out-plant factors, an old East-coast yard with fair community living conditions, and two yards in the same New England community under the same relatively bad out-plant conditions. Objective measures of performance were available in production and absenteeism figures. Fieldworkers themselves made observations of conditions within the plant and in the community. A cross section of workers was selected by taking every *n*th name from the personnel records, and then every worker so selected was interviewed in his home.

This study showed that in-plant factors were the most important determiners of production and worker motivation. By measuring out-plant factors it would not have been possible to have predicted the differences in production, whereas in-plant measures were good predictors. In other words, while community conditions of living were minor contributing factors, the main cause centered in the job itself — whether the worker had satisfactory earnings and promotional opportunities, good conditions of work, good supervision, and psychological rewards from the job he was doing.

When these criteria were met, the war worker could put up with considerable frustration outside the plant and still maintain a high degree of productivity.

These examples of the use of survey field methods clearly go beyond the early public opinion polling type of research. They are by no means the ultimate possible accomplishment of survey research outside the laboratory, but they suggest the possibilities both of getting applied answers to practical problems and of ultimately producing generalizations for the social sciences.

Among the many areas that can be investigated by the survey method is the whole field of group organization. The political scientists and the public administrators for a long time have been concerned with such matters as the amount of decentralization within an organization which will maintain the best group performance. The field of industrial production also presents problems that can be investigated by this method. What supervisory practices make for the best relations with workers? How valuable is authoritarian supervision, for example, because of the clarity and definiteness it provides? What is the relation between job security and the problem of earnings and ego-satisfaction? What are the ego-satisfactions that workers derive from their jobs which are especially important in job satisfaction and in productivity? What is the relation between the aspiration of the worker and his achievements over a period of time? What if he becomes frustrated in a job below his level of aspiration? Is there a habituation factor and how does it operate? The many problems in ego-motivation can be investigated through the survey method.

It is necessary, where possible, to supplement the survey method with actual field experimentation. Field experimentation, which will be discussed in the next paper,[4] is midway between the survey method and the experimentation of the

4 See Chap. 6.

laboratory; and the role of survey research can be very important in connection with field experimentation. The planning and design of field experiments can effectively utilize preliminary surveys of the situation and problems to be studied. Surveys can also be used for before-and-after measurements for action research. The effectiveness of an action program can be evaluated at any one point or any series of points in time.

In summary we may conclude that, when the survey method is used in a well-designed research plan, utilizing advances in techniques of sampling and data gathering and measurement, it has applicability beyond the limits of the public opinion poll. It will have increased usefulness as it develops and applies the logic of scientific experimentation outside the confines of the laboratory.

Chapter 6

FIELD EXPERIMENTS:
CHANGING GROUP PRODUCTIVITY

John R. P. French, Jr.

Associate Professor of Psychology, Research Center for
Group Dynamics, University of Michigan

IT is only in recent years that field experiments have come to play an important role in the methodology of social psychology. A field experiment is a research in which variables are manipulated and controlled in a life setting outside of the laboratory. To be sure, the practical social manager, whether an executive in industry or an administrator in government, often tries out new techniques of social management. Such tryouts for the purpose of improving results are not experiments; first, because they usually do not involve accurate measurement of the effectiveness of the new methods; and second, because they are not designed to discover the causes of the phenomena with which they deal. Usually the social manager has a hunch as to why a change in procedure will lead to improved results, but he does not have an explicit theory or set of hypotheses. He manipulates the social situation to find out *whether* a new method works and not *why* it works. A field experiment, on the other hand, is designed to test specific hypotheses and theories explaining social processes and social change. In order to do this, it must manipulate, control, and measure the relevant variables in the life situation with which it deals. In this respect the field experiment as a method of social psychology is related to the laboratory experiment.

Perhaps the best-known experimental studies of productivity in social psychology are the classical "alone-and-together" experiments. The experimental technique was the simple procedure of measuring the output of the individual alone, without the presence of others, and then comparing it with his output on the same task in a group situation. Some studies, for example, measured the individual's speed of tapping in isolation and compared it with the speed of tapping in a group of subjects all engaged in the same activity. In general these studies demonstrated that an indi-

81

vidual is more productive in a group setting than he is in isolation. However, they were not really measuring the productivity of a group as we think of the definition of a group in current research. In the "together" situations there was parallel individual behavior rather than interdependent behavior of members with differentiated functions. Thus the alone and together experiments were a transition stage from the study of individual psychology to the study of the psychology of real groups where the members are more highly interdependent and have a sense of belonging to an existing group.

The classical field experiments on group productivity are the comprehensive experiments conducted in the Hawthorne plant of the Western Electric Company. These experiments studied a real group in a factory where the members were, in fact, highly interdependent in their behavior. The original purpose of the experiment was to determine the relationship between physical conditions of work and the productivity of the group. Many months of careful measurement showed no significant relationship between output and such physical factors as temperature and illumination. The experiments did demonstrate in a dramatic way, however, the importance of social factors in group productivity. From a methodological point of view the most interesting of these findings was what we might call the "Hawthorne effect." In order to control more precisely the physical factors affecting production, the experimenters had set up a special experimental room for a small group of girls wiring relays. This bank-wiring room was separated from the rest of the factory and the girls working in it received special attention from both outside experimenters and the management of the plant. Careful studies of this bank-wiring group showed marked increases in production which were related only to the special social position and social treatment they received. Thus it was the social aspects of the experimental conditions set up for measurement which produced the increases in group productivity.

A more recent series of field experiments on group productivity has been conducted in the sewing plant of the Harwood Manufacturing Corporation in Marion, Virginia. These experiments were a logical development of the work of Lewin, Lippitt, and White on the effect of autocratic and democratic atmospheres on groups of children.[1] The autocracy-democracy experiments at Iowa were laboratory experiments designed specifically to explore the effects of different styles of leadership and of social atmosphere and organization on the behavior of the groups. They showed among other things that the democratic clubs of children were more productive in mask making than the autocratic clubs. In considering the significance of the greater productivity of the experimental democratic groups, two problems immediately arose: First, are these semiqualitative judgments of papier-mâché masks really adequate measures of productivity? Second, would democratic techniques induce greater productivity in a tough situation with adults such as in a factory? It is interesting to note that both these problems pointed to a field experiment as the best methodology for a next step in studying leadership techniques in relation to group productivity.

A sewing plant of the Harwood Manufacturing Corporation was chosen as the appropriate site for a field experiment because it provided exceptionally good measures of group productivity. In this particular factory the employees not only were paid on a piecework basis, but the output on all of the sewing jobs was measured in standard units of work determined by time and motion study. Since the unit is set by the same type of time study for all the many different

[1] Lippitt, R., and White, R. An experimental study of leadership and group life. In T. M. Newcomb and E. L. Hartley (Eds.), *Readings in social psychology.* New York: Holt, 1947. Pp. 315–330.

kinds of sewing jobs in the factory, we have a reasonably equivalent measure of output regardless of differences among jobs. Furthermore, the usual factory records provide measures of total output and of efficiency rating for every employee for every workday. Weekly average efficiency ratings are also calculated for each employee since the rate of pay is based on the efficiency rating for the week.

The early experiments in the factory were designed both to discover whether democratic techniques would be effective in increasing productivity in an industrial setting and to study more analytically the democratic methods. So the first step was to study the effect of one aspect of the total complex we call democracy — namely, decision making by the group rather by the leader. A series of experiments on the effect of group decision on production were carried out by Alex Bavelas, a psychologist who is also a skillful leader. In general the group decision procedure was as follows: Separate groups of women sewing-machine operators, usually ranging in size from four to a dozen employees, were taken from their machines for a group meeting with Bavelas in the management's conference room. The experimenter used a very friendly style of democratic leadership and went through such steps as talking about the greater ease of working together as a team, discussing with the group their previous individual production levels, questioning them about what level of production they might attain if they worked together as a team, asking them if they would like to set a team goal for a higher level of production, getting a group decision on the level of the goal and the time in which they would try to reach it. The experimenter was careful to leave all decisions up to the group, namely, whether they wanted to set a goal, and if so, at what level and in what time. In some of the groups no decision was made and there was no resulting influence on production. In most of the groups, however, the members decided to set a team goal to increase their production and specified the amount of increase and the time in which the increase would be made. In such groups the experimenter usually arranged for further meetings with the group in which they would check on how it worked out, and he would provide them with graphs show-

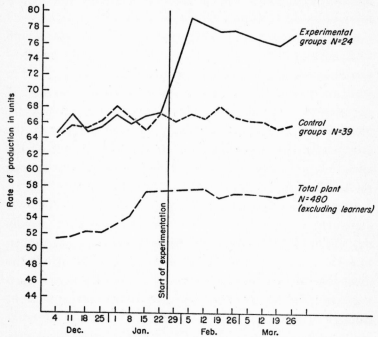

FIG. 6. Effect of group decision and pacing cards in a sewing factory.

ing changes in productivity for the group as a whole rather than for individual members. In some of these follow-up meetings, the groups which had reached their initial goal also set a second team goal to reach a still higher level of production.

The results of several such experiments are shown in Fig. 6. The bottom line of the graph shows that during the four months of the experiment, the average efficiency rating for the total plant varied between 52 and 58 units per hour. Both the experimental groups and the control groups were chosen from among machine operators who were definitely superior in production. The actual efficiency ratings of these groups are from 64 to 68 units per hour. In each experiment the control group was matched with the experimental group for the same type of job and for the same type of social setting and supervision. In all the control groups the level of production, as indicated by the top broken line, remained relatively constant over the four-month period. In all the experimental groups, on the contrary, there was a marked increase of production at the start of the experiment. The increase took place very suddenly in a period of a week or two and was maintained for over two months. This increase of about 18 per cent in production was accomplished without any changes in the job methods or other physical conditions of work. Thus the change is due to the leadership and the social factors involved in group decision.

In the same top curve for the experimental groups we have combined several groups where pacing cards were used. The two types of treatment have been combined in one curve because there are no significant differences as far as the results on production are concerned. In the experiments with pacing cards, the same friendly, democratic style of leadership was used, but a different aspect of democracy was employed in the procedure of the meetings. In general the supervisors in the factory urged the sewing-machine operators to sew as fast as possible at all times. The experimental technique with pacing cards was quite the opposite. The operators were permitted to plan their speed of work so that it varied from hour to hour. In the group discussion they talked about the effectiveness of variations in speed for ease of performance, and it was suggested that each operator should plan at the beginning of the day her speed for each hour, making sure to include some hours working slowly, some working at an average pace, and some working fast. No decisions to increase production were made in these groups. Nevertheless the results show a very similar increase in production.

Subsequently in the same factory, I repeated both the experiments using group decision and those using pacing cards on production, in addition to testing the effect of group decision on absenteeism and other problems of the factory. The initial results were very different from those of Bavelas. Fewer groups made decisions to increase production and those that did showed nothing like the amount of increase. Later, after I had had a year of experience in leading such groups, some of the group-decision experiments showed increases comparable to those in the figure.

As a result of all these experiments, three conclusions seem justified: First, the application of skillful democratic techniques of leadership in industrial settings can result in extremely marked increases in group productivity which will persist over long periods of time. Second, the procedure used, such as the difference between group decision and pacing cards, does make a difference, but this difference is not independent of the style of leadership. Third, in such experimental settings the style of personal leadership of the face-to-face group is probably the most important variable, and it differs markedly from one experimenter to another.

In all these experiments it had been necessary to make sure that the social conditions and the style of leadership used by the experimenter were not contradicted by the supervisors once the group was back in the work setting. For example, if an experimental group of operators decided to use pacing cards, it was necessary to instruct that supervisor not to press for faster production during one of the periods when they had planned to work slowly. The more general implications of these facts were clear: One cannot hope to change the level of productivity of the total factory by techniques of leadership on small subparts alone; it is necessary at the same time to change the institutional structure and patterns of the whole factory.

A different aspect of democratic group methods was studied in a recent field experiment in the same factory by Lester Coch.[2] In Coch's experiment the major variable was

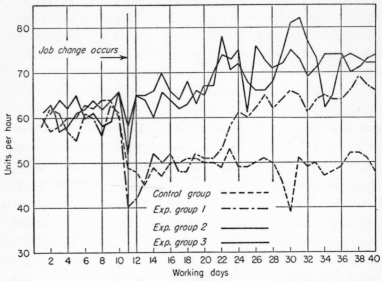

FIG. 7. The effect of participation on production.

democratic participation in deciding on changes in job methods. Figure 7 shows the effect of three types of participation on the productivity of groups. In this experiment, the practical problem of the factory management was how best to introduce changes in job methods in order to avoid the usual drop in efficiency. Normally in this factory when an experienced and efficient sewing-machine operator undergoes a change either through transfer to a new job or through alteration of her present job there is a very marked drop in production. Moreover, many experienced operators never

2 Coch, Lester, and French, John R. P., Jr. Overcoming resistance to change. *Human Relations*, 1948, 1:512–532.

recover to their previous level of efficiency even though the new job is no more difficult. Other studies have demonstrated that the low rate of production after transfer or job change is due primarily to social and psychological factors rather than to technical difficulties in relearning. Three variations in treatment were used to influence the social factors in the present experiment. All groups were matched for the difficulty of the job, for the amount of change in the job, and for the level of productivity before the experiment. The first group, or control group, was shifted by the normal factory procedure. This meant that the group was called into the conference room where they were given an explanation of why a change in job methods was necessary, what the new job would be like, and what the piece rates would be for the new job. They were permitted to ask questions about the change and full answers were given them. The lower curve in the figure shows that this control group dropped from a level of about 60 units per hour before the change to about 50 units per hour just after the change. This lower level was maintained for a period of thirty days following the change or until the group was broken up. For experimental group one, a greater degree of democratic participation was used. Not only did they receive more detailed and dramatic explanations of the need for change, but the group chose representatives to participate in designing the new job, setting the new piece rate, and later in training the remaining members of the group. This procedure resulted in enough feeling of participation on the part of the representatives so that they spoke of the new job and the new piece rates as "our job" and "our piece rates." The second line on the graph shows that the average production of the 13 operators in experimental group one dropped even more than the control group, namely down to 40 units per hour. However, it recovered much more rapidly and in a period of fourteen days had again reached standard. During the remaining days the group continued to improve, achieving a production level higher than their productivity before the experiment. The third type of treatment was given identically to experimental groups two and three. Every member of these somewhat smaller groups took part directly, not through representation, in the same procedure used with only the representatives in experimental group one. That is, all members of the group received an explanation of why the change was necessary, and participated in designing the new methods and setting the new piece rates. The results for these two groups under a total participation technique are indicated by the top two lines on the graph. On the first day after transfer, they dropped down in production but not nearly as much as the other groups. On the second day, they had already achieved their former level of productivity and for the remaining days they continued to show an increase in production, reaching a level of approximately 15 per cent higher than their production before the change.

Not only was the productivity after change of the three types of groups proportional to the degree of participation, but the amount of aggression expressed against management and the turnover rate also varied inversely with the degree of participation. Thus we see that greater participation leads to both greater productivity and greater satisfaction in the group.

We have already noted in the Harwood studies one example where a series of field experiments grew out of a laboratory experiment. On the other hand, the reverse is often true in social psychological research: One field experiment will give rise to a series of several more analytical and more highly controlled laboratory experiments. What, then, is the relationship between field experiments and laboratory experiments in the methodology of social psychology? As we look back at both the laboratory experiments and the field experiments on group productivity one fundamental fact is clear: Logically the two methods are similar in that both are experimental methods which reveal the basic dynamics of groups through the control and manipulation of relevant variables. In the life setting as in the laboratory, this control can be achieved through the selection of groups, through experimental designs using matched groups, and through actual manipulation where experimental procedures are applied in a controlled way. As compared to other methods in social psychology, both laboratory experiments and field experiments have the advantages of greater analytical power in disentangling the many variables involved in social behavior, more conclusive interpretation of results, and more definite proof of causal relationships.

The main difference between laboratory experiments and field experiments is that the latter are guided not only by the research objectives but also by the practical objectives of the group being studied. For example, the dominant objective of industry is production and this objective cannot be subordinated to the research objectives of a field experiment. The freedom of the field experimenter is limited to those types of experiments which do not conflict with the goals of the organization with which he works. This does not mean that real experiments cannot be done. Rather it means that the researcher must be flexible in choosing appropriate problems to study in field settings. Most fundamentally, it means that he must render a service which helps the practitioner to achieve his practical objectives. Thus the experimenter must have the special skills of the consultant in order to solve his methodological problems of control and measurement.

Some of these specific practical problems of conducting field experiments can best be illustrated by a recent study done by the Research Center for Group Dynamics.[3] This experiment on changing group productivity was conducted

[3] Bradford, Leland, and French, John R. P., Jr. (Eds.). The dynamics of the discussion group. *Journal of Social Issues*, 1948, 4 (2).

under a contract with the Office of Naval Research and in cooperation with the National Education Association and several universities. In contrast with the industrial studies we were concerned primarily with studying intellectual productivity. We wanted to determine the effects of personality factors on the productivity of group thinking and planning of the type that occurs in a staff conference or in most committees. At the same time we wanted the content of the group thinking to center on problems of human relations.

In order to produce experimental changes in the productivity of such group thinking we chose a training setting, where a controlled, experimental treatment could be used. The most practical setting for studying such phenomena seemed to be a brief training workshop. From the very beginning the joint planning of the workshop was guided by two purposes: the research objectives, and the practical training objectives. A three-week curriculum centering on human relations skills was mapped out by a faculty of expert trainers. Sixty-five paying delegates were selected to attend. They included top leaders from government, industry, education, and social service organizations. All of them had positions of major responsibility in regard to human relations.

The first major problem of experimentation was the control of the situation through the design of the experiment. The research staff planned jointly with the training faculty, giving due consideration to both the research objectives and the service objectives of the training. A fairly high degree of experimental control was achieved. In the first place, it was possible to divide the delegates into five comparable groups matched for occupational background, sex, and power position in the delegate's own organization. Second, a special group composed of representatives from each of these five groups was created for intensive clinical study of the influence of personality on group functioning.

Even more important was the experimental treatment applied to all the five groups. The training faculty readily agreed to use the same basic curriculum and similar training techniques for the purpose of producing specified changes in the functioning of the groups. This control through experimental treatment is still in its infancy in social psychology. The types of skills and techniques most needed for such group experiments are human relations skills and leadership techniques. Experimenters must develop the ability to produce large enough changes in groups to be measured by the crude instruments now available in social psychology. In this sense, we have few good technicians in social psychology today. Consequently, the experimenter must either develop his own skill or rely on the skills of more expert practitioners. In this workshop we took the second course by using already skilled trainers as experimenters. For some time to come field experiments will be able to exert stronger experimental influences and produce greater changes by using expert practitioners.

In studying the productivity of the groups at the workshop, it was clear that three different levels of measurement would be required. In the first place, we needed a measure of the productivity of each of the five matched subgroups in terms of its output and the efficiency of its process. These measures of the subgroups were obtained by standardized productivity test situations, given at the beginning and at the end of the workshop, and by continuous observation of the process of group interaction. In the second place, the productivity of each of these training groups was partly a matter of the degree to which the individuals in the group learned the basic human relations skills. Thus a second measure of productivity was the change in individual skills, ideology, personality adjustment, and goals. In the third place, the workshop was thought of as an isolated temporary subculture, and definite procedures were planned for influencing the cultural patterns, such as the style of objectivity, the permissiveness, the institutional organization and structure, and so on. Thus adequate study of group productivity required a third level of measurement, namely the institutional level.

It is clear that we were attempting both control and measurement at the level of the individual, at the level of the subgroup, and at the level of the total institution. In effect, we were approaching the problem of changing group productivity from the point of view of individual psychology, from the point of view of group psychology, and from the point of view of cultural anthropology. Consequently we needed a large and varied staff including experimenters, clinical psychologists, social psychologists, and anthropologists. The total number of personnel in this complex research team was 35. Not all field experimentation will require such a large and varied staff; yet it is clear that the more complex problems, like group productivity, can be most effectively tackled by a team.

One of the most significant lessons to be learned from this experiment is that a truly amazing degree of cooperation with practitioners can be achieved. Both the faculty and the delegates devoted much time and energy to research either as subjects, as data collectors, or as experimenters. The comprehensive measurement program and the control of the training situation were possible because the participants became involved in the research process. In addition they received a valued service from the research team in that some of the data were analyzed immediately and the results were presented to both the faculty and the delegates. This immediate feedback of information helped to improve the training process and to accomplish the training objectives.

In the light of these examples, what conclusions can be drawn about the methodology of field experiments?

First of all, recent studies have demonstrated the possibility of scientific field experiments with a relatively high degree of experimental control and accurate measurement. Through cooperation with the scientist, the rough tryout of the social manager can become a truly scientific experiment. For the social psychologist such a field experiment opens up new and important areas as research problems. Furthermore, through cooperation with skilled practitioners, he can supplement his ability to manipulate and control variables in an experimental design. Where the research has applied purposes, the problem of generalization is reduced, for the study can be conducted on the actual social problem in its real social setting.

Second, we can begin to see the requirements for conducting field experiments in cooperation with practitioners: careful selection of appropriate problems and field settings, experimenters skilled in cooperating with others, involvement of practitioners in the research process, and a service relationship of the researcher to the practitioner.

The practical and applied values of field experimentation are even more definite. They can give the most clear-cut and easily understood answers to the human problems of the social manager. For the social scientist this means that the problem of applying the results of his research are greatly reduced, for he no longer has the difficult job of selling practical administrators on the value of applying his findings. The administrator has already seen it proven in his own organization and that is sufficient. Moreover field experimentation is peculiarly adapted to discovering the kinds of macroscopic laws in social psychology which can be applied to the control and change of social problems. The experimenter, like the social manager, must be action-oriented. In approaching a problem like group productivity he must consider the methods and techniques for change as well as the reasons for the present state of affairs. Naturally, therefore, his results will have important applications to practical problems.

For handling the more complex problems, such as group productivity, we will continue increasingly to use larger research projects requiring a team approach. Such research teams in the future will consist more and more of scientists from different disciplines, such as psychiatry, psychology, social psychology, sociology, and anthropology, and of the practical social managers in our leading institutions. Thus the integration of the social sciences as subject matter and the integration of research personnel into cooperative research teams is an important step if we are to meet the challenging social problems of today.

Chapter 7

A COMPARATIVE STUDY OF NATIONAL CHARACTERISTICS

Donald V. McGranahan

Lecturer on Social Psychology, Department of
Social Relations, Harvard University

and

Ivor Wayne

Department of Social Relations, Harvard University

Dr. McGranahan's work on this study is part of a research
program made possible through a fellowship from the John
Simon Guggenheim Memorial Foundation. Published in
Human Relations, 1948, I: 429–455. Reprinted by permission.

I

I F Germans and Americans have not behaved alike in recent years, this may be because of differences in immediate circumstance, or because of differences in basic psychological traits ("national character"). Empirically, there is no
way to find out how Americans would have behaved if
subjected to all the circumstances to which Germans were
subjected ten or twenty years ago. We cannot plant the
American people in the middle of Europe at a given historical date, immerse them in German surroundings, and then
see if they would react like Germans to the same stimuli.
In fact, we could not logically equate external circumstances
for the purposes of comparison without making Germans
and Americans alike in the first place, since one important
external circumstance influencing any given individual is the
nature of the personalities of those about him. We can try,
however, to rule out the influence of *temporary* circumstances, such as the National Socialist regime, by comparing
peoples at successive periods of history. If we find that certain differences between Germans and Americans actually
endure through variations of historical circumstance — if
these differences turn up in the more propitious years of the
Weimar Republic, as well as in the pre- and post-Weimar
days — then we shall have much firmer ground for arguing
the theory of national character. Such a theory need not
imply stereotyped uniformity within a nation. We are concerned only with the statistical distribution of psychological
traits. Nor need it imply racism. Enduring and distinctive
traits may depend upon basic social-environmental conditions that persist with relatively little change through the
ups and downs of political and economic fortune.

The following study is an experimental attempt to compare German and American traits reflected in the 45 most popular plays in each country in 1927. This was, in each country, a year of relative prosperity and of political democracy. The theaters were free to produce what they pleased and the audiences free to attend what they pleased. In Germany, inflation had ended, production had made a phenomenal recovery, the Locarno Conference had eased the international situation, and the National Socialists numbered but 40,000. The German political leader of the time was Stresemann, a representative of conservative liberalism, free enterprise, and private property — a man not uncongenial to the Republicans who were then in political control of the United States. In the election of 1928 (which year must also be considered, since the popularity of plays produced in the latter part of 1927 was based on performances running into 1928), the Social Democrats were victorious with the largest representation they had achieved in the *Reichstag* since 1920.

A smaller sample of popular German and American plays from the period 1909–10 has also been used for comparison. This, too, was a relatively prosperous period in both countries, but Germany differed politically in that it was an empire under the Kaiser. In this earlier period, however, there was no recent military defeat to distinguish the German situation from that of the United States.

Our first assumption in this study is that popular drama can be regarded as a case of "social fantasy" — that the psychological constellations in a dramatic work indicate sensitive areas in the personalities of those for whom the work has appeal; their needs, assumptions and values are expressed ("projected") in the drama. The successful play must be attuned to the audience. There can be no claim that dramatic material reflects the total personality of the individual who enjoys it. Analysis of popular songs, poetry, art, humor, novels and short stories, propaganda, advertising, religious writings, public activities, statistics on crime and mental dis-

301.1504

ease, etc., may well reveal other psychological facets of a historical population that is not accessible for direct study.

Our analysis of the plays is clearly limited by the fact that the playgoing audience is not a proper sample of the national population. It represents primarily an educated, urban segment. However, the German and American audiences are roughly comparable. If significant psychological differences can be shown between corresponding segments of two national populations, then this indicates a difference in national character, unless one rejects a statistical definition of that concept and reserves it only for nationally uniform traits. Whether the traits expressed in the plays actually extend to other parts of the population must be determined by study of other sources. The German and American playgoing audiences are not, of course, exactly comparable — for for example, New York (Broadway) has a greater role in the American theater than does any metropolis in Germany where the theater has been more decentralized. Furthermore, seats in the German theaters have tended to be cheaper. This is connected with the important fact that the German theater, unlike the American theater, has been primarily under public ownership, or subsidy from public funds. These considerations must be borne in mind in the evaluation of our results. Sym

II

As a first step in choosing the sample for each country, all reported productions for the calendar year 1927 (including productions first staged in the last weeks of December, 1926) were examined, and musical comedies, operas, revues, and follies were eliminated. From the remaining plays, which relied on story content and characters for appeal, were eliminated all revivals and all foreign importations, so far as these could be determined. Austrian, Sudeten, and Swiss-German plays were excluded from the German sample. This left about 135 first productions ("tryouts") for each country.

An attempt was then made to select the 45 most popular plays in each country. In the United States, popularity was judged on the basis of (1) success on Broadway, as measured by the recorded number of performances;[1] (2) success in the rest of the country, as indicated by the frequency and content of reviews in theater journals and local newspapers;[2] (3) over-all success as indicated by various "end-of-the-season" discussions, tabulations, and over-all reviews.[3] In the case of the German plays, popularity was judged on the basis of (1) the success of the play in spreading through the theaters in the various German towns, as indicated by the speed with which reviews of the play followed each other in special theater periodicals, the over-all frequency of such reviews, and the estimate of popular reaction therein contained;[4] and (2) over-all success as indicated by retrospective summaries, etc.[5] No single objective measure being avail-

[1] Given in Burns Mantle. *The best plays of the year, 1926/1927;* and *The best plays of the year, 1927/1928.*

[2] Publications consulted for relative success outside of New York were: *ibid.; The Theatre; The Theatre Arts Monthly; Variety; Commonweal; American Mercury* (articles by G. J. Nathan); the Theatre section of *The New York Sunday Times;* local newspapers in Boston, Chicago, Los Angeles, San Francisco. The clipping file of the Harvard Theatre Collection was found especially useful for our purposes.

[3] Seasonal reviews of the American theater were taken from sources cited in the preceding footnote.

[4] German publications consulted were: *Deutsche Rundschau, Deutsches Volkstum, Literarischer Handweiser, Die Literatur, Preussische Jahrbuecher, Das Schauspiel, Die schoene Literatur, Sueddeutsche Monatshefte, Das Theater, Westermanns Monatshefte.*

[5] For German retrospective summaries and seasonal reviews, the publications in the preceding footnote were consulted, *Das Theater* being especially useful; also *Thespis Almanach 1930,* and Frels, W., Die deutsche dramatische Produktion 1927, in *Die schoene Literatur, 29.*

able for a play's national success in the case of either country, it was necessary to combine criteria in estimating the
order of rank in popularity. The procedure ensured that all
recognized successes were included. For the less successful
plays, it became increasingly difficult to assess relative order
of popularity (the total selection was limited to 45 plays in
each country rather than an intended sample of 50, because
at about this point the plays were becoming uniformly and
indistinguishably unsuccessful).

Once the 45 plays for each country were chosen, summaries of their contents were written down. The summaries
were based upon a reading of the play or of an abridged
form of the play as given by Burns Mantle, or upon an examination of several independent reviews, since a single reviewer could not be relied upon to give an adequate digest.
An element of unconscious bias may have crept into the sum-
marizing of some of the plays, although a careful attempt
was made to obtain accurate digests. The summarized contents were then subjected to various types of analysis by
three judges.[6] There is no established psychological method
of content analysis in handling dramatic material. The three
judges independently gravitated toward categories that followed the traditional lines of breakdown in drama: the
nature of the setting, of the central characters, of the plot,
and of the conclusion. An attempt was made by each of the
judges to use the categories employed in the Thematic Ap-
perception Test, but the material did not lend itself easily
to this type of analysis. A method seemed required by
which each plot could be treated as a unit. Furthermore,
exploratory attempts at analysis indicated that it would be
wiser to let the categories emerge from the material so far
as possible rather than to superimpose categories.

It was found that the structure of nearly all the dramas

[6] Mr. Arnold Meadow kindly assisted the authors in this preliminary
analysis.

could be described in terms of the pattern of conflict — the interplay of opposing forces — that underlay the plot: conflict between youthful lovers and parents, between honest folk and criminals, between revolutionary and reactionary political forces, between moral and immoral impulses within the individual, etc. Once the patterns of conflict in the different plays were established, it was further found that these conflicts could be classified into six major groups or categories, designated as (1) the love theme, (2) the morality theme, (3) the idealism theme, (4) the power theme, (5) the career theme, and (6) the outcast theme. These major categories were then defined in some detail according to their typical ingredients (the definitions are given in the following section).

In view of the ease with which prejudice and preconception operate in the field of national psychology, it was felt that the judgments of the two authors should not be the sole basis for determining German-American differences in terms of these categories, since the authors knew which plays were German and which were American. For this reason, seven additional judges were used.[7] The summaries of the plays were arranged in a random order, and authors and titles were deleted. A number of the German plays were already set in the United States, England, Russia, or some other non-Germanic country and had non-Germanic characters. These summaries were left in their original form. In the case of the remaining German plays, the settings and the names of the central characters were transformed into American settings and names, with but five exceptions: in one case, a French setting was substituted; and in the remaining four cases the

[7] The seven judges were two graduate students in the Department of Social Relations at Harvard University, two Nieman Fellows at Harvard University, a professional anthropologist, a college graduate studying for the theater, and a well-educated German refugee.

German settings and characters could not be changed without changing the basic content of the play. To offset the latter situation, four American plays were given German settings and names. The seven independent judges were then provided with the 90 summaries (each summary averaging a third of a single-spaced typewritten page in length), the detailed definitions of the basic themes, and directions to classify a play under a given thematic category "only if the theme is central to the plot; that is, if the theme could not be eliminated without significantly changing the essential nature of the plot and leaving it logically or psychologically incomplete. If a love theme, for example, is merely thrown in for incidental interest, this is not to be counted." Subjects were told a play might contain either one or several of the basic themes.

In addition to this thematic analysis, the judges were asked to classify each play "according to whether the ending is (1) happy, (2) unhappy (tragic), or (3) ambiguous (mixed); also according to whether the play is primarily *personal* in content and import (concerned with private affairs of individuals), or primarily *ideological* (concerned with political, social, national, or international issues)." Subjects were told that the purpose of the experiment was to test the reliability of the categories used.

Each of the authors also classified the plays independently, so that there were nine judges all told. In computation of the results, a play was reckoned to fall under a given category if five or more of the nine judges agreed in placing it there. In only 7 of the 90 plays did the majority fail to find any one basic theme applying. There is no standard formula for measuring the reliability of categories of content analysis such as were used in this study, but inspection of the data indicates that the love theme and the idealism theme were employed with the greatest agreement among judges, the morality and power themes with least agreement.[8] For example, when the majority of the judges agreed on the presence of the love or idealism theme in a given play, this majority was more often a majority of all nine of the judges than a majority of eight, seven, six, or five judges; whereas a majority agreement in the case of the morality and power themes was more frequently a majority of only five or six of the judges. Agreement on the level of action (personal vs. ideological) and the nature of the ending of the play (happy, unhappy, ambiguous) was also fairly high, in the sense that when there was majority agreement, it was most frequently universal agreement.

In the statistical results presented, the procedure of defining the presence of a given category by the majority agreement of the nine judges applies only to the data on the basic themes. In the case of the level of action, and the nature of the endings, the results represent majority agreement among only seven judges (because of pressure of time, two of the judges were not asked to use these categories). All other data represent the analysis of the two authors only, and can be distinguished by the fact that they are presented in numerical form, not in percentages.

III

The following are the detailed definitions of the basic themes as given to the judges who analyzed the plays.

The Love Theme

This category includes only heterosexual love of the boy-girl, husband-wife, master-mistress variety. It does not include family love — unless incest is clearly indicated — or love of any nonsexual object. However, plays dwelling on

[8] The relatively high reliability of the idealism theme was due in part to the fact that in some of the plays the hero was explicitly named an "idealist" by the playwright.

the problems of married people in getting along with each other are to be ordinarily included, even if romantic love is not highlighted. In plays falling under the love theme, dramatic interest usually centers about the question whether two lovers, or potential or would-be lovers, will be united in the end. Opposed to the love relationship may be any number of factors: parents, personal misunderstandings and grievances between the lovers, career ambitions, character defects, higher ideals of one form or another. These forces must be overcome or reconciled before the happy union can ensue. Love may, of course, lose to any of the forces conflicting with it.

The Morality Theme

Plays built around a morality theme deal with the problems that arise from the moral standards of society and human weakness or sinfulness in falling below these standards. Morality is used here only in the sense of *conventional personal* morals such as are treated in the Bible and in Western criminal law. We are not here concerned with good and bad philosophies of life, political faiths, or social systems, but with specific individual behavior. Typical immoralities or sins are: personal crimes of any sort, individual dishonesty, sexual looseness, intentional injury to other persons. Opposed are such virtues as: law-abidingness, honesty, "true love," kindness, and consideration of others. The good and evil forces may be represented externally by good and evil men (*e.g.*, honest folk and criminals) or internally by good and evil impulses. In plays with a basic morality theme, as here defined, the moral is assumed to be the conventional, the expected, the normal behavior of the social majority; the immoral is the deviant, the behavior of the man who falls below the social norm. Indeed, the moral is often treated as having the force of society and perhaps even of "nature" behind it, while the immoral is unsocial, unwholesome, and unnatural. Ordinarily, in plays with a basic morality theme, the guilty person who falls below the social norm must either *reform* (*i.e.*, readjust to society and nature) or *suffer punishment* (*or both*). The play clearly implies the superiority of virtue, both as desirable and as necessary. Finally, it is assumed in these plays that the choice between good and evil paths of actions is a matter of free choice between possible alternatives, that the individual is therefore responsible for his morality or immorality. Plays of the morality type may be said to provide the spectator with a certain excitement by dramatizing immoral impulses; but at the same time they provide him with a moral lesson to the effect that "crime does not pay." Because nearly all plays involve crimes or immoralities of one sort or another, it is desirable to define the morality type negatively and to indicate the kinds of play that do not fall under this category: first, plays that present illicit love-making as charming or amusing and involve no moral judgment, no character reform or punishment fall only under the love theme; second, plays that justify an ordinarily immoral or criminal act in the name of a higher ideal or value (patriotism, "liberalism," art, etc.) or treat ordinary morality as petty and narrow in comparison with the hero's higher vision, or present a hero who stands far above a corrupt and evil world, fall under the category of idealism; third, plays that present merely a primitive conflict in which moral forces play no role fall only under the power theme; fourth, if the central character is a criminal or other deviant type and the play presents him sympathetically, or makes it clear that he is not responsible for his sins (society or fate is responsible), then the play belongs under the outcast theme.

The Idealism Theme

Plays featuring the idealism theme have a central character who is consciously attempting to pursue a set of high principles. He may be a revolutionary idealist or a humanitarian idealist; a devoted supporter of the old regime, a nationalistic patriot, or an internationalist; a freethinking liberal, a priest, or an art-lover. The important point is that his motives and his character set him apart from, and above, the masses of the people. He is not merely seeking to live an average, conventional, private life, and he does not behave in a manner that can be expected of the average citizen. In the pursuit of his principles, he may have to sacrifice some conventional personal value — his reputation, his life, love, social acceptance, personal happiness, normal creature comforts. He may very well commit some act against conventional morals. The idealist theme is thus concerned with the conflicts engendered by those who stand above the ordinary, the morality theme with conflicts engendered by those who fall below the ordinary. Unlike the moral individual, the idealist usually has convention and normality arraigned against him. Idealism plays often imply the desirability of reforming society as a whole, of redefining values, or of preventing a social change that is under way. The idealist typically has to fight against materialism, conventional moral scruples, self-interest, prejudice, pettiness, stupidity, weakness of character, personal desires, lesser loyalties, conflicting systems of ideals. These forces may be external or within himself. Included under idealism are plots that stress an extraordinary sense of duty, loyalty, or patriotism, or single-minded devotion to a cause.

The Power Theme

The power theme deals with the problems that arise from the conflict between two individuals or groups for the same object, territory, position of authority, or controlling influence over a situation. It includes personal conflicts for power, class conflicts, ideological conflicts, revolutions, war, etc. Also included are plays in which a central character seeks power against such obstacles as his own inferiority or his more tender impulses. Frequently the struggle involves the use of violence, ruthlessness, trickery, or coldbloodedness on the part of one or both adversaries. In power conflicts, the more powerful side usually comes to dominate the situation but it is not necessarily the better side that wins — in fact, the reverse is true if the worse side is stronger. Plays that are principally constructed and resolved in terms of who is right and who is wrong, or who is good and who is bad, do not, of course, fall under the power category. Power may be represented by a number of different factors: physical or material means, strength of character, ruthlessness of purpose in pursuit of a goal, lack of "soft" emotions, courage, cunning, trickery.

The Career Theme

In career themes a central character is attempting to win personal success in his occupation, to make money, create a work of art, or advance his professional status. The goal is personal achievement, not the success of an ideal, system, way of life, nation, or other superindividual institutions. Various obstacles may block the path to success.

The Outcast Theme

In a number of plays we find as a central character a person who is placed outside normality or normal society by some handicap, abnormality, inferiority, or stigma. This may be a physical handicap — deformity or extreme ugliness or illness; a mental handicap — some form of mental disease; a political handicap — the condition of being an exile; or any one of a number of social handicaps, such as being a criminal, prisoner, outlaw, vagabond, pauper, Negro, bastard, prostitute. The play dwells upon the relationship of this person to normal society, his reactions to society or society's reactions to him. It may show, for example, how he seeks normal love and acceptance, how he reacts with cunning or brutality to his outcast status, how he is not himself responsible for his status, how society misunderstands and abuses him. Sometimes the outcast has a superior perspective and is also an idealist. *If a criminal or other outcast is the central character of a play, the play ordinarily falls under the outcast theme.* But if the central character is clearly a normal individual and the criminal is his adversary, representing evil forces, then the play is to be classified under the morality theme, since the interest here is not portraying the problems of the outcast, but the conflict between good and evil. Not included in this category are plays in which the suspicion or accusation of, say, murder, is falsely attributed to innocent persons, and the action of the plot is centered about revelation of the true situation. The outcast status must be real, recognized as such by both society and the individual. Plays are not included in which a person, nominally a deviant, enjoys popularity because of his deviance.

IV

The results of this work are shown in the following tables. Table 1 indicates the percentage of plays in each national group falling under each of the basic themes, as defined by a majority of the nine judges. American plays, it can be seen, are primarily concerned with love and personal morals. The German plays are considerably more preoccupied with idealism, power, and the problems of the abnormal or outcast. Little difference appears in personal career themes.

The love and morality themes often go together: 10 of the 20 plays that contain morality themes (American and German combined) were also scored as having love themes. Similarly, idealism and power tend to go together: 5 of the 16 plays considered to express power conflicts were also considered to contain the idealism theme.

TABLE 1. THE BASIC THEMES*

	United States		German	
	Number	Per cent	Number	Per cent
Love..........	27	60	14	31
Morality.......	16	36	4	9
Idealism.......	2	4	20	44
Power.........	1	2	15	33
Outcast........	0	0	8	18
Career.........	5	11	4	9
No agreement..	6	13	1	2

* The totals add up to more than 100 per cent because of the fact that a single play might be classified under several categories. It should be recalled that the 45 plays from each country do not represent a random sample, but the total population of all plays above a certain level of popularity. One can, however, examine the significance of the German-American differences in frequencies in Table 1 by using the simple chi-square technique recommended by Snedecor (Snedecor G. W. *Statistical methods.* 1946. P. 26). So far as morality, idealism, power, and outcast themes are concerned, the differences are significant on the 1 per cent level; the love category difference is significant on the 5 per cent level; the difference in the career category is not significant.

Table 2 indicates that the German plays are strikingly more preoccupied with social and political problems than are the American plays. Their level of action is primarily ideological; the basic conflict is between forces that represent divergent social, political, or economic interests, or divergent philosophies of life. The problems portrayed in the American plays, on the other hand, are overwhelmingly personal — love affairs, family affairs, difficulties and hostilities on a nonideological level. The German ideological emphasis is obviously tied up closely with the emphasis on the idealism theme.

The German plays also have more unhappy endings than

TABLE 2. THE LEVEL OF ACTION

Action level	United States	German
Ideological.................	4%	51%
Personal....................	96	47
No agreement..............	0	2

do the American plays (Table 3). Connected with this is the fact that the side of virtue consistently wins out in the American plays, but the unsympathetic side often comes out on top in the German. Frequently in the German plays the central character is a ruthless, treacherous, or egotistic individual who wins success because of these very qualities.

The German central characters tend to be older and are more often males than is the case in the American plays (Table 4). More noteworthy than these statistics, however,

TABLE 3. THE ENDINGS

Type of ending	United States	German
Happy......................	67%	40%
Ambiguous..................	24	29
Tragic or unhappy...........	9	27
No agreement...............	0	4

is the difference in the type of woman who plays a central role. When a female carries the burden of the plot in American drama, she tends to possess in eminent degree qualities that are considered feminine — beauty, emotionality, charm, tenderness, softness, motherliness, etc. But when a female is the central character in a German play, she tends to be a strong, aggressive type of person — she defeats men in economic competition, ruthlessly exploits male weakness, rejects lovers who have too soft a character, refuses to give way to love because this would interfere with her more serious purposes, etc. In short, femininity as such may be as important as masculinity in the American plays, but is rarely so in the German plays, where female equality of importance seems to be possible only by achievement of masculine qualities and values.

In keeping with the fact that more of the German plays are on a social level, a further distinction is at once apparent — the German central characters are more frequently social types; that is, their social status or role plays an important part in the logic of the plot. They behave as they do because they are proponents of a cause, princes, rulers, generals, political functionaries, exiles, typical representatives of a social class, etc. The American central characters, on the other hand, are more "ordinary people" whose role or status has less critical bearing on the plot — their occupation could be changed without basically altering the plot. The social

TABLE 4.   THE CENTRAL CHARACTERS

Types of characters	United States	German
Sex:		
Male.....................	19	33
Female..................	15	9
Couple (male and female)...	6	0
Larger mixed group........	5	3
Age:		
Youthful................	23	13
Middle-aged or elderly.....	13	19
Indeterminate or mixed.....	9	13

type that seems to be favored as the central character in the American theater of 1927 is the entertainer or artist, although the detective-policeman and the man of great wealth also turn up.

On the basis of what the authors and critics in their respective countries called "light" and "serious" plays, there was no national difference in relative frequency. In both countries the ratio was approximately two light plays to three serious plays. This ratio also holds if we consider not the specific samples chosen but the total number of dramatic productions in each country in 1927. Marked differences appear, however, in the time and place of the action presented in the plays (Table 5).

The figures reflect a German predilection for historical plays. Seventeen plays out of our sample, and 34 per cent of the total German drama production in 1927, fall into this category. But the German drama also takes leave of the contemporary domestic scene in legends and fantasies and

in foreign settings.   One curious result is the fact that in
the year 1927 more plays on the subject of American history
were produced in Germany than in the United States.   The
German departure from the contemporary scene, however,
must not be taken as evidence of a flight from current social
problems.   It indicates rather a German tendency to view

TABLE 5.   TIME AND PLACE OF ACTION

Time and Place	United States	German
Time:		
Contemporary (1920–1927).	42	23
Historical		
1789–1919.	1	7
1453–1788.	1	9
Antiquity.	1	1
No specific time: sagas, fairy		
tales, symbolic fantasies. .	0	5
Place:		
Domestic setting.	41	26
Foreign or legendary setting	4	19

these problems *sub specie aeternitatis*.   Such plays seem
designed to have a deep meaning for the present.[9]

V

Not only do the German plays differ from the American
plays in the percentages falling under the various basic
themes; German plays under a given theme also differ in
specific content from the American plays under the same

[9] A German dramatic critic explains this phenomenon in the following terms: "The German is essentially a believer in history. History is
authoritative; it clarifies events, even today's events. Historical drama
remains important as long as out of present events the mythos of our
times has not been created; *i.e.*, as long as the material data of our
days, their human and 'real' characteristics, do not attain a superindividual, universally valid form, and as long as this form has not
been cast into a comprehensive expression anchored in eternity." Lipp-
mann, H. Die Frage des deutschen historischen Dramas. *Die Literatur,*
1929, 29:618*ff.*

theme. German love plots differ from American love plots.
The patterns of conflict found in the United States plays
with a basic morality theme are not the patterns found in
the German morality-theme plays; and so with the other
major categories.

The Love Theme

TABLE 6. PATTERNS OF CONFLICT IN THE LOVE THEME*

Love conflicts	United States	German
Youthful love vs. parents	8	0
True love vs. unwholesome love	8	(1)
Love vs. temporary misunderstandings	6	0
Love vs. ideals, higher values	0	4
Idealists' love vs. social norms	0	2
Power conflicts for love	0	3
Love vs. outcast status	0	2
Miscellaneous	6	3

* The totals do not add up to the exact number of plays classified under
the love theme because a few plays appeared to have more than one
pattern of conflict.

There are three types of love plot in the American plays
that can be fairly easily identified.

The first presents a pattern of conflict between youthful
lovers, on the one hand, and parents who oppose or interfere
with this love, on the other. The parents are usually pictured
as well-meaning but ill-advised individuals, who do not want
to lose their sons or daughters; but sometimes they appear
immoral, even criminal, in their opposition. A father may
murder (Abbott and Bridgers: *Coquette*) or attempt to
murder (Brooks and Lister: *Spread Eagle*) his daughter's
suitor. A mother, unfaithful to her husband, may vie with
her daughter for a young man (Stone: *Restless Women*).
Possibly related psychologically are several American plays
in which a criminal individual in a position of authority
threatens to break up youthful love — the half-mad sea
captain in *Fog* (by Willard) who tells the young lovers they
are half brother and sister. So commonly understood is the

idea of youthful love's flourishing under parental opposition that we find a popular American play, *Tommy*, in which love is temporarily blighted by parental approval. An outline of this play is given below, following two other examples of youthful love vs. parents.

Cushing: *Devil in the Cheese*. Mr. Quigley, an archeologist, takes his family with him to do some digging around a monastery, and hopes thereby to lose Jimmy Chard, who has been pursuing the daughter, Goldina. But Goldina is rebellious, and Mr. Quigley wishes he could see what is in her mind. When he eats a piece of cheese dug up with an ancient vase, he gets his wish. The spirit of the cheese takes him inside Goldina's head and he realizes how much in love and how incurably romantic she is. When he wakes, and Jimmy is the only one with wit enough to save the party from bandits, Mr. Quigley is glad to welcome him into the family.

Howard: *The Silver Cord*. Mrs. Phelps attempts to break up the relationships between her son, David, and his wife, Christina, and between her younger son, Robert, and his fiancée, Hester. It is marital love vs. mother love. The situation is argued in a legalistic manner. In the end David follows Christina, leaving mother and house forever; but Robert and Hester are separated.

Lindsay and Robinson: *Tommy*. Marie Thurber really loves Tommy Mills, but because her family so obviously wants her to marry him, she turns for relief to Bernard, a salesman. To save the situation, Uncle Dave, the town's political boss, wisely decides to oppose Tommy, and is so successful that the family throws Tommy out. Then Marie flies to Tommy's defense, and the happy union ensues.

The second common type of love plot in the United States plays concerns a hero or heroine who is faced with an inner conflict and must decide between wholesome "true love" on the one hand, and unwholesome false love on the other hand (*i.e.*, love based on mere sensuality, thrills, money, security, prestige, love outside the marriage pattern, etc.). The plot builds up to the act of decision: If true love is chosen, the ending is happy; if not, or if the decision comes too late, there is punishment and suffering. These plays are preoccupied with the problem of sexual immorality, but in the end teach the lesson that one ought to be good. The following are typical:

Kelly: *Behold the Bridegroom.* Tony Lyle is one of the social butterfly set. She has had a lingering engagement with one of the boys in her circle, but when Spencer Train is introduced, Tony realizes he is her ideal. He is the first man to disapprove of her, and she feels her newborn love is hopeless; but she dismisses her fiancé and tells him there is another. The boy goes to his club and shoots himself — one cause of Tony's collapse. She has discussed the matter of Train with her cousin, Eleanor. She confesses affairs with other men. The realization that she cannot go to Train as wives should go to their husbands becomes an obsession. Only when Train visits the suffering girl is there hope for their romance to bloom. In a beautiful scene, she tells of herself and the great change in her character. The curtain finds Train wondering whether the bridegroom has not come too late.

Rogers: *Her First Affair.* Ann Hood, eager for the full test of life at twenty, is convinced she must have an affair or two before she is ready for marriage. She picks on Carey Maxon, a freethinking novelist, and, left alone with him by Mrs. Maxon (who knows her husband well), assumes a scanty costume and a provocative manner — without result. This adventure, however, serves to excite Brian Cutler to action, and Ann elopes with this eligible suitor.

Glenny: *New York Exchange.* Ernest, a promising young tenor, is loved by Sally Parks, a musical comedy star, but his affections are stolen by Ella May Morton, an aging lady with a passion for youthful companionship. Ernest finally breaks his bonds, refers to his patroness as a "philanthropic louse," and returns to Sally.

The third type of love plot that would appear to have captivated the American audience involves a pattern in which two lovers or potential lovers become estranged through some misunderstanding or petty annoyance, and the problem of the plot is how to effect emotional readjustment and bring them happily together again at the end. Included here are stories of the boy-meets-girl, boy-loses-girl, boy-wins-girl variety; but husbands and wives, too, are frequently separated and reunited in the American plays. The circumstance that causes the friction varies from play to play: relatives, financial difficulties, minor or suspected infidelities, occupational success of one of the lovers. The lovers usually become reconciled because one of them (or sometimes both) is persuaded to a change of mind by some dramatic circumstance, such as a slap on the face, an act of special ingenuity, a sudden danger, sickness, or an accident to the other. One example of this type will suffice.

Anderson: *Saturday's Children*. On the advice of her sister, Bobby Halevy traps Rims O'Neill into a marriage proposal. They really love each other, and he gives up a long business trip to get married. But six months later wedded love has been pushed aside by grocery bills, curious relatives, disillusionment. Bobby realizes something is wrong. Her sister's advice now is to tie Rims to her with a baby. But Bobby has another idea. She returns to her old job and takes a furnished room by herself in a house so respectable that the doors have to be left open when gentlemen call. Some time later we see Bobby in her room. The window slowly opens; Rims sneaks in behind her back, goes over to the door, and locks it from inside. Bobby kisses him — they have found each other again.

It is a striking fact that no German play of 1927 with a basic love theme falls clearly into any one of these three common American classes. There is no case of youthful lovers in conflict with parents. Perhaps the closest is the story of an illegitimate son of Odysseus, Telegonos, who competes for Penelope along with Telemachos and the other suitors, but eventually slays both Odysseus and Penelope, thereby becoming king of Ithaca (Fischer: *Das Meer*). Here it is the son who interferes with love between the parents. There is, however, one German play in the sample of the 1909-10 period portraying youthful love vs. parents — *Hilfe! Ein Kind ist vom Himmel Gefallen,* by Schmidtbonn. It merits special attention here.

A burglar breaks into the home of a rich industrialist and, instead of taking gold and silver, robs the daughter of her virginity. The daughter becomes the mother of a child, and eventually joins the burglar, whom she loves. Together they blackmail the father. The father gives in and offers to take the hero into his industrial enterprise. But, loving each other dearly, and refusing to submit to the petty, narrow ideas of the older generation, the youthful couple emigrate to America instead; and it is implied that the hero will become a leader of men on the new continent.

It should be noted in this play that the young lovers are guilty of serious breaches against conventional morality (robbery, promiscuity, blackmail) while the parent represents social norms of respectability; yet the rebellion of the young couple in a sense becomes justified because they have a broader view of life; conventional norms are narrow and mean. We shall see in other German plays to be discussed, particularly under the idealism theme, that rebellion against existing authority is portrayed as immoral according to conventional ethics; it is not justified in terms of personal rights, yet it may be justified in terms of a higher and broader vision.

There are several German plays of 1927 that picture ideal-
istic-romantic lovers in rebellion, not against parents, but
against petty-bourgeois norms in general. In the name of
modern "liberalism," religious mysticism, or some other set
of values superior to those prevailing, lovers find a basis for
lasting unity. In Ilgenstein's *Skandal um Olly*, love succeeds
only when it overcomes the narrow attitudes of society
toward illegitimacy. The determined heroine tests the
hero's broad-mindedness by pretending to have an illegitimate son, provoking a scandal in the town and exposing
widespread hypocrisy. The child that the heroine pretends
is her own is actually the hero's illegitimate son; the hero
comes through with flying colors, and she finally marries him.
German plays in which lovers are united by common ideals
merge into plays which portray the idyllic unity of lovers
in some natural or "lyric" setting. In *Schinderhannes*, by
Zuckmayer, a rough but chivalrous Robin Hood of the Rhine-
land lives in a state of idyllic woodland love with his natural
wife (who bears him a son). He is finally caught and hung
by the petty burghers.

But if lovers are united in German plays because they
embrace a common value system superior to conventional
norms, it is also true that love may fail because it comes into
conflict with higher values and ideals. An ardent feminist
gives up love for the sake of her cause (Berstl: *Dover-Calais*).
In several cases, such as *Knechtschaft*, by Schulz, love comes
into conflict with patriotism, and one lover becomes the
cause of the other's death.

German plays in our sample do contain the "eternal tri-
angle," but this is not, as in the case of the American plays,
presented as a problem of *moral choice* between wholesome
and unwholesome love. The one possible exception (Schef-
fler: *Das Land im Ruecken*) tells a gloomy tale of two
brothers who have committed a brutal murder, one of them
now married to the former fiancée of the murdered man.

The other brother demands money or a night with the wife (who has actually slept with him once in the past for a sum of money). Husband and wife confess their sins, but this proves no solution. Finally, seeking punishment, the husband gives himself up, and the wife strangles the blackmailer in order to follow her husband.

Usually in the German plays with love triangles, two men are vying for one woman, and it is the competing men whose actions resolve the conflict, which becomes often a power conflict. In Langhof's *Knock Out*, the contestants resort to foul means against each other and both are eliminated. Consistent with the fact that the German emphasis is not upon the dilemma of moral vs. immoral choice in love is the further fact that both contenders for a woman may represent about the same degree of rightness or wrongness, or at least they are not primarily distinguished as true and false lover. If the situation is not resolved as a power conflict, it may be resolved on the basis of devotion to higher values, *on the part of the men*. For example, in Kaiser's *Papiermuehle*, a husband gives up his wife in the name of art:

Ollier, literary critic, is engaged in studying and reviewing the works of Duchut, a famous poet and dramatist. Ollier is especially fascinated by the passion of Duchut's drama, "Francesca da Rimina." The poet is a "sober and cool individual" under normal conditions, the reviewer reasons. He decides that he will try to find the soulful mistress of the poet who inspired the work. At length he discovers that "Helene," the personified inspiration, is his own wife, who during a summer vacation met the poet regularly in an old paper mill. Moved by generosity, he determines to leave Helene to the poet. In the final act the two men get together in a businesslike fashion to settle all questions arising from Ollier's decision. The paper mill, *i.e.*, Duchut's literary production, must go on.

The German audience would seem to be relatively little interested in the problem of how couples are to readjust and reunite once a point of friction has developed; at least, there are no German plots of the popular American variety in which lovers become estranged, then kiss and make up. On the other hand, there are several German cases, but no American examples, of love that is complicated by the abnormality or outcast status of the central character (illustrations of such plays are given under the outcast theme). In both German and American plays there are a few cases where

TABLE 7. PATTERNS OF CONFLICT IN THE MORALITY THEME

Morality conflicts	United States	German
Conflicts from immoral love impulses...............	5	0
Immoral parent vs. youthful love..................	2	0
Law or honest folk vs. criminals..................	8	0
Miscellaneous......................................	2	4

love is complicated by career ambitions, or by the fact that one of the lovers is a delinquent. In general, the American lovers end up in each other's arms in the overwhelming majority of all plays containing minor as well as major love themes. Statistically, however, the chances do not seem to favor the final union of German lovers.

The Morality Theme

As already indicated, the morality theme frequently appears in union with the love theme. It often appears as a minor theme in love plots where the judges did not consider it important enough to receive an independent rating. Under the morality theme fall also a number of American plays in which detectives, policemen, ordinary honest folk (brothers and sisters, young couples in love, kindhearted elders) are pitted against evil men — crooks, gangsters, corrupt attorneys, criminal maniacs, etc. The evil side consistently has the initial advantage but the side of virtue is consistently triumphant.

Veiller: *The Trial of Mary Dugan.* Mary Dugan, professionally known as Mona Tree, of the Follies, has been found staring at the dead body of Edgar Rice, the man with whom she has most recently been living. Her clothes are blood-smeared and her fingerprints are on the dagger with which Rice has been killed. At her trial the evidence is all against her, when her young brother, Jimmy, arrives from California. Being a lawyer, Jimmy objects to the way in which Mary's lawyer is conducting the case, the lawyer resigns, and Jimmy takes over. He now learns for the first time of his sister's mode of life and of the sacrifices she has made to pay for his education. He defends her passionately, and finally twists the testimony of the state's own witnesses into an admission of guilt.

Cormack: *The Racket.* The play starts with a dull night at a police station on the outskirts of Chicago, to which Captain McQuigg has been transferred because he interfered with the operations of Scarsi, a bootleg czar who wields more political influence than the boss of the town. Scarsi has come into the same district with a brewery. One of the cops brings in Scarsi's young brother, picked up in a stolen Rolls Royce. The gangster replies by walking into the station house and shooting the cop who arrested the brother, then making his getaway. He is captured and brought back. The battle now takes the form of a fight between the captain to hold his man and a corrupt administration to "spring" him. The captain finally outwits the crooked district attorney and gets his man.

In *The Trial of Mary Dugan* there are actually two morality components: the problem of the innocent vs. the guilty and the problem of the heroine's sexually immoral private life. The latter was motivated by kindness to her brother, and the audience can be sure she will reform after the trial. The American plays will forgive, on occasion, immoral or illegal acts that spring from a "good heart." There are several American plays featuring a tough, semilegal character with a heart of gold.

One thing that stands out in the American plays is the emphasis given to character reform as the solution to the basic problems of human conduct. The central character who has sinned usually reforms, taking a new and wholesome attitude. Criminals frequently reform. The alternative is certain defeat and punishment. Two American plays are in large part devoted to the problems of reformed criminals (one of the plays on which the judges could not reach a majority agreement, *Four Walls*, by Burnet and Abbott, is of this type). Or criminals may confess at the very end and thereby assure the happiness of the hero and heroine. Plays stressing character reform merge into those in which there is a less fundamental change in personality, but in which, nevertheless, a change in attitude of some individual or group is a critical part of the plot. For example, parents who oppose young lovers may change their attitude, realizing that they were ill-advised in their opposition, or a husband may realize that he has been neglecting his wife. (Note the attitudinal change involved in nearly all the American plays summarized above under the love theme.) Such change hardly deserves to be called character reform, and plays of this kind do not fall under the morality theme, yet they illustrate a basic principle that underlies a great many American plays — the principle that the solution to conflict and difficulties in life can be obtained through personal reorientation. The individual's capacity to change often provides the basis for happy endings. It should be noted that in the case of United States plays featuring murder trials, an impartial tribunal of justice when presented with persuasive evidence changes its mind as to who is guilty. Furthermore, once a delinquent has suffered and reformed, then society must recast its attitude toward him and welcome him back.

Fannie Hurst's *It Is to Laugh* features both character reform of a petty criminal and attitudinal change toward the reformed criminal.

Of the four German plays classified by the judges under the morality theme, none has the clear-cut opposition between moral and immoral forces that is found in the American plays. In two of them (*Das Land im Ruecken* and *Knock Out*) both sides to a conflict share heavy guilt and sin. In the other two, murders are committed, but not out of serious criminal intent. In one case, a Junker ex-general with a delicate sense of family honor shoots his daughter for sleeping with a communist, but the daughter was in fact dutifully trying to obtain important documents for her father (Sternheim: *Das Fossil*). In the other, four townsmen caught in a chain of circumstances successively appear to kill a hunchback, but he revives at the end (Halm: *Das kleine Bucklige*).

By and large, the German central characters do not reform or change their minds in the way of solution to the basic dilemmas of life. Criminals do not reform. In five of the six cases where criminals play important roles in the German plays, they are unreformed yet more or less sympathetic characters who battle not virtue and decency, but smug, petty society. There are, it is true, a number of German plays in which men who have sinned confess their crimes at the end, but in no case does the confession make either the guilty party or anyone else happy. It merely confirms the certainty of punishment, sometimes adding a touch of self-immolation to the general gloom.

The German plays have several ways of dealing with the problem of personal sin or crime. (1) The responsibility for a crime may be removed from the perpetrator and placed upon society as a whole, which should do the reforming. We find, for example, a play in which a poverty-stricken woman who has murdered her crippled and cynical husband is portrayed as not responsible for this act; rather, the social system that forced a sordid slum life upon her is held responsible (Jung: *Legende*). Similarly, a pair of anarchist idealists who derail a train are shown to be more or less innocent victims of an evil social system (Schaeferdick: *Moerder für Uns*). Plays of this nature shade into plays in which some physical abnormality explains an individual's criminal behavior. (2) An act against conventional morality may be reinterpreted as a courageous, praiseworthy act in terms of a new set of values. There is a strong current of

TABLE 8.   PATTERNS OF CONFLICT UNDER THE IDEALISM THEME

Idealism conflicts	United States	German
Idealist vs. external obstacles: ruthless materialists, egoists, ideological enemies, mass stupidity, Philistinism..............................	2	15
Idealist vs. internal obstacles: personal love, loyalty, softness of character.........................	0	5

protest in the German plays against conventional values that are considered petty, narrow, mean, and confining — what the Germans like to call "Philistinism." (3) Conventional sins, like murder of a beloved person, while not condoned as such, may be justified under the tragic necessity of fulfilling a noble ideal. (4) Finally, the good man who faces powerful forces of evil may, overwhelmed, fall into a state of apathetic resignation or commit suicide.

The Idealism Theme

According to the 1927 plays, where the American is a moralist, the German tends to be an idealist. In his pursuit of high ideals, the German hero comes into conflict with two sorts of obstacles: those arising from without, and those arising from within, his own personality.

The most striking pattern of conflict in the German plays of 1927 presents a social or political idealist opposed by ruthless, materialistic forces.

Unger: *Goddins Ewige Masken.* Faso, idealist and dreamer, discovers a land so fertile it could feed a whole nation. But to this land comes Goddin, in his "eternal masks" as millionaire, shipowner, usurer, business agent. He leases the land for its gold deposits, and lures over Faso's friends with his money. Faso, having lost the fight, concludes that the promised land is a dream of the future.

Gurk: *Wallenstein and Ferdinand II.* Wallenstein does not want war; but aspires to a great German Reich that will become the leader of a peaceful development of the world. He believes in astrology and in his mission to make Germany great. But failing health impairs his energy, and in the course of the drama his downfall is brought about by ruthless, unscrupulous enemies — courtiers, Jesuits, Ferdinand's secretaries — whose interests are for themselves rather than for the greatness of Germany. After Wallenstein's murder, the weak, well-meaning king breaks down completely.

Paquet: *William Penn.* William Penn sets up an ideal state in America, but his selfish enemies in England intrigue against him. He is thrown into jail; and in the debtor's dungeon he meditates upon human meanness and dies in melancholy.

Lilienfein: *Freiheit wider Willen.* The heir apparent of a small state upon returning from France transfers power to the people, who are in revolt. But the leaders of the revolution are stupid; the base and ruthless courtiers crush the revolution and set up a double for the real prince; the latter seeks spiritual freedom in exile, declaring that the real revolution cannot be expected before a hundred years.

In several of the German plays classified under idealism, the idealist is opposed not so much by selfish, materialistic interests, as by the stupidity, narrow conventionality, or Philistinism of the masses, who fail to appreciate higher values. This latter conflict provides the basic pattern in:

Johst: *Thomas Paine.* The spiritual leader of American freedom goes to France and joins the Revolution, only to discover that its slogans have become empty. He tries to save the king for the sake of human ideals, for even a king can understand the elevating feeling of human equality if accepted by the community. But the masses do not understand Paine. The king dies, Paine is imprisoned. After seventeen years of suffering, he returns to America to discover his friends dead and his name forgotten. Needed no longer, he throws himself into the Delaware. His songs of freedom, however, perpetuate his spirit in the youthful republic.[10]

There was only one American play in 1927, although a very popular one, that approximated the German conflict between humanitarian idealism and ruthless materialism.

Sherwood: *The Road to Rome.* Amytis, Grecian wife of Q. Fabius Maximus, home from a shopping trip, hears of the invincibility of the barbarian forces now at the gates of Rome and decides to visit Hannibal at his headquarters. She crosses the Carthaginian lines, and is brought before Hannibal as a spy; she then uses her charm to convince him that war can only conquer territory, not eternal values, and that the gods were deceiving him in favor of the merchants of his home town when they sent him out to subdue Rome. There is a higher value than conquest — humanity, the hu-

[10] Paine did not, of course, die by throwing himself into the Delaware. For that matter, William Penn did not die in a debtor's prison; the real Count Pahlen lived for many years after the assassination of the Czar; and Wallenstein, far from being an idealist without personal ambition, was quite the opposite. The German playwrights are not peculiar in distorting history to fit the demands of their dramatic conception: Hannibal was not dissuaded from an attack on Rome by the charm and humanitarian reasoning of Amytis, as the American play *The Road to Rome* would have it.

man equation, which a truly great man must find. Hannibal is charmed and persuaded, and later withdraws his forces.

Note that in this play the tender humanitarianism of a woman defeats the ruthless forces of war and materialism. This is possible because an individual in a critical position, Hannibal, was open to persuasion and underwent a change of attitude. Sherwood's popular *Road to Rome* provides an interesting comparison with the play that was apparently the most popular production in Germany in 1927:

Neumann: *Der Patriot.* Count Peter Pahlen, the Prime Minister of Russia and the most powerful figure at the Court, realizes that the mad Czar, Paul I, must be removed for the sake of Russia and the Russian people. He plots a revolt. The Czar senses that disaffection is spreading and appeals for protection to Pahlen, "his only friend." Pahlen advises abdication but when the Czar refuses, standing on his dignity, Pahlen arranges an assassination. While the attack is on, Pahlen stands with a loaded pistol ready to kill the attackers should they fail, and to reaffirm his loyalty to the Czar. They succeed, and Pahlen commits suicide to show that he inspired the revolt out of unselfish patriotic motives.[11]

In this story idealism and ruthlessness are wedded. The Patriot, for the sake of a higher ideal, murders his friend and master whom he could not persuade. This is not a conflict between good and evil, although the moral issue is critical; the conflict is between ordinary decency and extraordinary patriotism. It is in such conflicts that one often finds the German sense of tragedy.

[11] Because of its popularity in Germany, *Der Patriot* was translated into English and staged on Broadway. It failed after eight performances. Pahlen's readiness to reaffirm his loyalty to the Czar reminds one of the behavior of the German officers after the failure of the Putsch of July, 1944.

In order to succeed in this world, the German idealist must exercise great "strength of character," which often means that he must overcome tender personal sentiments of love and affection. Several German plays portray conflict between patriotic idealism and personal love. Others directly point to the moral that a weak or soft character spells failure.

In Welk's *Gewitter über Gottland,* the union of ruthlessness and idealism is even more pronounced than in *Der Patriot.* Members of a communistlike religious sect living

TABLE 9. PATTERNS OF CONFLICT UNDER THE POWER THEME

Power conflicts	United States	German
In relation to idealism...........................	0	5
In relation to outcast status......................	0	4
Miscellaneous power conflicts.....................	1	6

on an island catch a self-seeking betrayer of their ideals through the aid of a prostitute; the traitor is dragged through the streets, pilloried, then delivered to the merchants of Hamburg for execution.

The Power Theme

The power theme is implicit in most of the German plays of 1927 classified under idealism, and five plays were considered by the judges to feature equally the idealism theme and the power theme. The power theme also turns up in a number of German plays in which the central character is an outcast, oppressed by some stigma or inferiority, who compensates for his status by striving for power or dominance. But we find other central characters as well, who are beset by a strong drive to achieve power as a goal, sometimes with apparent approval of the dramatist, as in *Geld,* by Brentano; sometimes with apparent disapproval, as in:

Unrah: *Bonaparte*. This play describes the conflict between Napoleon's egoistic ambition and the elements in him making for human greatness. The Duke of Enghien, the last Bourbon, stands before him, erect and cool, awaiting his verdict. Will Napoleon prove to be not only the greatest politician, diplomat, and soldier of his time, but also the greatest man? He could afford to be generous. He will not. Napoleon fears the Duke as a potential representative of royalist legitimacy. He decides that the Duke must be judged by the (Napoleon-dominated) tribunal at Vincennes. In the meantime, Hulin, the hero of the 14th of July, senses the grave peril of Napoleon's egoism. The Republic is in danger! Repeated warnings by reliable Republicans against the mirage of personal glory go unheeded by Napoleon. Hulin, therefore, decides to have Napoleon murdered by the Duke at the Vincennes trial, in the interests of the Republic. At the trial, however, the Duke provokes a violent argument by expounding his philosophy. He is beaten by the wild Republicans, sentenced to death, and shot. When Napoleon later encounters resistance among the Republican generals, he uses brutal force and unscrupulous intrigue to attain his goal. Triumphantly he proclaims himself Emperor of France. The play ends with Hulin's prophetic words: "There is a germ of death in this triumph. Your face is that of marble statues, of copper coins, of plaster — a dead man's face!"

We also find assorted power conflicts between individuals, social classes, or nations in the German plays. For example:

A grouchy old writer gets into an argument with a small-town grocer, feels insulted, and sues him. The grocer buys and bribes witnesses left and right, defeats and drives out of town the unpopular writer. The grocer becomes the town's hero and is named its citizen of honor. (Schirmer: *Der Ehrenbuerger*.)

Characteristically enough, the only American play judged to have a basic power theme concerns a conflict between a young man and the father of the girl he loves, the older man attempting unsuccessfully to get the younger one killed. Those individuals in the American drama who seek dominance or employ ruthless techniques are consistently outwitted, in contrast to the German exponents of ruthless power.

The Outcast Theme

TABLE 10. PATTERNS OF CONFLICT UNDER THE OUTCAST THEME

Outcast-theme conflicts	United States	German
Physically abnormal person vs. normal society.......	0	4
Criminal or other socially abnormal person vs. normal society..	0	4

In the German plays of 1927 that contain idealist-heroes, the majority of these idealists become exiles (*i.e.*, outcasts) or suicides at the end. Some, moreover, start off as weak, sickly, or abnormal. For example, in Toller's *Hoppla, Wir Leben*, the idealist-hero comes from an insane asylum, witnesses the corruption and materialism that has overcome the revolutionary party in which he participated, returns to the asylum, and commits suicide. In addition to such plays, there are eight German plays in which the theme of the outcast or abnormal person in conflict with normal society quite dominates the plot. These plays are primarily concerned with showing how the condition of being an unloved outcast or abnormal results in criminal, violent, ruthless, or power-seeking behavior on the part of the outcast; or how society itself is heartless in relation to the outcast.

Schaeferdiek: *Moerder für Uns.* Two young anarchists have caused a catastrophic train derailment. The play shows how their anarchistic attitude has been produced by economic, social, and political conditions — and by their feeling of not belonging anywhere. They have an obscure, metaphysical, "ideal goal," and commit crime partly for money to realize this goal. When they see the dead victims, they give themselves up and accept the death sentence.

Geyer: *Grenadier Felsing.* A soldier in Frederick's army has been emasculated and lives platonically with his wife. The rumor of his secret gets about, and to spike the rumor he arranges to have a cavalry sergeant sleep with his wife and beget a child. But during the execution of the plan, overcome by a fit of jealousy he rushes into the bedroom and stabs the sergeant.

Feuchtwanger: *Die Petroleuminseln.* Deborah Gray, the "Lady Ape," is excluded from normal social intercourse by her inhuman ugliness. She runs a vast trust in a South American archipelago, aggressively and efficiently, the equal of all the businessmen she meets. But with one of these men she falls in love. He laughs at her, she becomes desperate, her business reaches a crisis. But Deborah successfully rejects personal feelings, purges her enemies, and proceeds with cold brutality to achieve material success once more.

Society's relation to an outcast may be portrayed in a serious, socially conscious production, but it may also be featured in a light and humorous dramatic production. In *Der dreimal tote Peter,* an ex-galley slave and vagabond is three times thought dead in the course of his escapades with respectable society, on one occasion being stabbed on the stage; but he escapes to the open road in the end. (German dramatic humor of 1927 appears to have a considerable amount of blood and murder. Four of the comedies contain a total of eleven real or pseudo deaths. In the American drama, murder tends to be reserved for the more serious morality plots.)

The Career Theme

Although there is little difference between the number of German and American career themes, it should be noted that the German plays place career ambitions primarily in a context of power seeking or inferiority compensation (*cf.* *Die Petroleuminseln* above); while the American plays connect career ambitions primarily with love problems (career success may either upset or ensure love), and, to a lesser extent, with moral problems and with revolt against family authority.

V

Samples of German and American plays in the 1909–10 period were examined to check on the possibility that the differences found in the 1927 plays may have been due largely to the German defeat in the First World War, and the distress that followed. It was possible to locate only 17 popular plays for each country in this older period. Hence our conclusions in this category must be rough and tentative.

The German predilection for historical plays and plays with a foreign setting is maintained in the older period, with almost exactly the same ratios. The German preference for masculine central characters is likewise maintained, and such females as occupy the center of the stage are strong and manlike. A somewhat smaller proportion of the older German plays, in comparison with the 1927 plays, appear to be ideological in nature and unhappy in outcome; but the German-American differences in these respects are still apparent. So far as the basic themes are concerned, the picture remains much the same with regard to German-American differences in morality, idealism, and power. There are relatively more German love plots in the older period, but also more American love plots, so that the German-American difference is consistent. The outcast theme appears less sharply defined in the older German plays, though it is still present to a greater degree than in the American plays. One striking change, however, is found

in the much larger proportion of older American plays that
fall under the career theme (there is no change in the German plays in this respect). We find a number of American
dramas in which a young man from a country town goes to
the big city to win success, falls in with evil companions (*e.g.,*
actresses), but eventually overcomes temptation and returns
to his native town to achieve success there and marry the
girl he has always loved. (Horatio Alger stories were popular in 1909–10.)

In the American plays of 1909–10, we find the same conflict between wholesome and unwholesome love, but the
conflict between youthful lovers and parents is less pronounced; and there is a greater tendency for the parents to
be morally right in such conflicts, as in stories of the prodigal
son who associates with bad women against his parents' desire. The same general American tendency to structure
personal conflicts in terms of right and wrong is apparent,
and likewise the tendency to resolve conflict through character reform or change of attitude. In the older German plays
we find the same conflict as in 1927 between love and patriotism; also the same plot concerning two men of art who love
the same woman but become firm friends because they love
art more (the wife in this case commits suicide). The conflict between moral and immoral impulses (or individuals)
figures no more prominently in the older German plays than
in the 1927 plays. As in 1927, acts that are contrary to conventional personal morals tend to be justified or excused
because the perpetrator is a person of high ideals, broad
vision or great strength of character, capable of going beyond the petty strictures of conventional morality.

Consider the following list of heroes and heroines in the
German plays of 1909–10: a minister's husky daughter who
seduces a university teacher she likes but then, although
pregnant, refuses to marry him because he turns out to have

a weak character; a strong-minded young lady with modern ideas on feminine equality and free love, who has a child by a married architect, flaunts convention and petty bourgeois laws, and is happily united with her lover in the end; Cesare Borgia, pursuing the goal of uniting Italy and making his family a ruling dynasty, who murders his brother and his sister's husband and forces his father, the Pope, to absolve him; an old emperor, retired to America with the wife of his palace commander, who returns to the throne to fight a revolution brought on by his incompetent successor, and in the course of the fight sacrifices the life of his own son for the empire; the burglar who robs the daughter of a rich industrialist of her virginity, is joined by the daughter to blackmail the father, but when successful refuses to enter the father's enterprise with its petty ideas and instead emigrates with the daughter to America; a duke who lives illicitly with a red-haired countess when he is not defeating the Huns, and is rewarded for his strength and courage by becoming the first king of Germany, eventually marrying a proper blonde; an individualistic nobleman who tests the love of his cowgirl wife by having her undress while he embraces a society lady (the wife is chased out of the castle but comes back later and they live happily forever after). German concern for greatness of character is well illustrated in one older play where a King of Persia is disturbed by the noble character of his Vizir and, to test the servant's greatness, attempts to seduce the Vizir's wife; but the Vizir offers his wife to the King, and later, when his life is pardoned by the King, refuses to accept the pardon; whereupon the King, outdone in greatness, commits suicide.

The older German plays reveal one important difference from the German plays of 1927. In the latter we have noted a frequent pattern of conflict between a tender idealist and a strong, ruthless materialist, the latter winning out. In the older plays, however, idealism and ruthlessness are more frequently wedded, and the tender humanitarian is rarely a hero. We find, for example, a play in which the hero is a ruthless Junker who drives off a weak, idealistic neighbor, but who marries the idealist's daughter when she proves to be a strong character herself, strong enough to resist his advances and point a gun at him. The old emperor who kills his son and Cesare Borgia who kills his brother are examples of the ruthless idealist, similar to the 1927 "Patriot" who killed his Czar. Even ruthless idealists, it must be noted, frequently die in the end; although their deaths are not presented, on the surface at least, as a moral lesson teaching the wrongness of their action, but as part of the tragedy of life. The German idealists of the 1909–10 plays tend to be more often national idealists and less often humanitarian or revolutionary idealists than those of 1927.

VII

The data of this study show clear differences between the German and the American drama, and lend support to the theory that there are real and persistent German-American psychological differences — or, if you will, differences in "national character." But it is still possible that our results are due to certain peculiar factors in the drama situation. For example, German public ownership or subsidy vs. American private ownership may be the explanation. This question can only be settled by other types of evidence. In favor of a broader interpretation of our results are the following considerations:

First, the results are consistent with German-American differences found historically in other realms, such as philosophy and politics.

Second, the results of the present study are consistent with other comparative studies of Germans and Americans, using other types of data.[12]

Third, a limited check on our United States play data is offered by the study by Dorothy B. Jones of 100 American films in 1941–42.[13] Jones used a different method of analysis, attempting to isolate the "wants" of the central characters, but certain of her results permit comparison. She found that 68.1 per cent of the central characters of the films primarily wanted "love," while we found that 60 per cent of the American plays had basic love themes. The other categories of wants found in the films (fame, reputation, or prestige — 26.1 per cent; safety — 15.9 per cent; a way of life — 13.8 per cent; money or material goods — 9.6 per cent; rightness — 9.0 per cent; etc.) do not correspond to any of our molar categories of analysis of the dramatic plots. Our morality theme, for example, might include plots in which the central character primarily wanted reputation, safety, or rightness. But it should be noted that these wants that Jones found are primarily personal rather than ideological. Of all major characters in the films 61.2 per cent "were indulged with respect to all their 'wants' at the end of the picture," 10.1 per cent were wholly deprived. Our data show that 67 per cent of the American plays of 1927 ended happily, 9 per cent ended unhappily. Of the central characters in the films 33 per cent were female, not far different from the plays. In general, where the evidence permits comparison,

[12] Cf. especially: H. S. Lewin. A comparison of the aims of the Hitler Youth and the Boy Scouts of America. *Human Relations*, 1947, 1:206–227; and D. V. McGranahan. A comparative study of social attitudes among American and German youth. *J. abnorm. soc. Psychol.*, 1946, 41:245–257.

[13] Jones, Dorothy B. Quantitative analysis of motion picture content. *Public Opinion Quarterly*, 1942, 6:411–428.

it points to a much higher degree of similarity between the United States plays and the United States films than between the latter and the German plays.

Fourth, the general principle that German and American playgoing audiences do have different likes and dislikes is supported by independent data. During the occupation period, various plays from the American stage have been presented in German theaters. Experience has shown that a number of these productions have been popular in both countries; some, however, quite popular in the United States have been poorly received by German audiences, while still others that achieved relatively little success in this country have turned out to be hits in Germany. For example, a recent report [14] indicates that *Boy Meets Girl*, a success in the United States, has been a failure in postwar Germany, while *Thunder Rock*, the English story of a man who retires to solitary existence in a lighthouse because of his dissatisfaction with the present world, has achieved considerably greater popularity in Germany that it did in the United States.

Fifth, during the war, a series of American motion pictures (about 15 in all) were pretested on 200 to 300 German prisoners of war.[15] Although the prisoners were selected anti-Nazis, it is interesting to note their reactions and their major criticisms of the American films. In general, the majority considered the American films they had seen to be inferior in content to German films. (*a*) The foremost criticism was their lack of "depth," their superficiality, their failure to penetrate into the more profound and meaningful sources of human action. Films like *Christmas in July*, *My Sister Eileen*, and *The More the Merrier* were condemned

[14] *The New York Sunday Times*, Dec. 21, 1947.

[15] These studies were carried out in England in 1944 and 1945 by the Surveys Section of the Office of War Information under the direction of Dr. Elmo Wilson. Dr. Wilson very kindly supplied us with the data here summarized.

as "superficial trash." Only 8 per cent of the prisoners liked *My Sister Eileen* very well; 2 per cent liked *The More the Merrier* very well; but 72 per cent liked very well the socially significant *Tales of Manhattan*. (*b*) Closely related was a second major criticism — that the American films were "unnatural," "unreal," the developments of the plot and the actions of the characters were quite improbable. Artificial happy endings also came in for criticism. In connection with our finding above, that the German plays have less emphasis upon character change or attitude change than do American plays, it is instructive to consider the reaction to the film, *All That Money Can Buy*. This film is based on Benét's story, *The Devil and Daniel Webster,* in which the oratory of Daniel Webster persuades a fantastic jury of American traitors to release a farmer from his pact with the Devil. It was liked for its Faustian theme and its condemnation of materialism (the farmer signed over his soul for material success). Yet the film as a whole was relatively unpopular. "The chief objections raised took the form that changes in ethical outlook on the part of some of the characters were not established reasonably, and were too abrupt. Thus the psychological preparation of such changes seemed unconvincing, over-simplified, and naïve." Prisoners complained that the film was "too moralizing," unrealistic, un-German. (*c*) The anti-Nazi prisoners disliked the way in which love relations and sentiment were handled in a number of American films, preferring the more soulful sentimentality of the German approach. *Seven Sweethearts* seemed to express this latter approach and was very well liked by 86 per cent of the subjects. This picture gives a warm and peaceful portrayal of life in the idyllic setting of a Dutch-American village, dealing with the hotelkeeper's seven beautiful daughters (one slightly spoiled), their devotion to their father, their romances, and their multiple wedding. By way of contrast, *Mr. and Mrs. Smith* was relatively unpopular. (This is a farce in which a couple discover their marriage was not legal, and become separated, the wife resuming her maiden name — with numerous attendant complications.) (*d*) The German prisoners objected strongly to the crime motif when it turned up in American films. For this reason, they did not like *Shadow of a Doubt*, the story of a conflict between a pretty girl in a small town and her friendly appearing uncle who is in fact a vicious criminal from the big city. They specifically objected also to the more incidental treatment of crime in *Here Comes Mr. Jordan, Tales of Manhattan*, and *Moontide*. (*e*) They objected to the emphasis upon materialistic values and money-making in such pictures as *Christmas in July*. (*f*) The personality and behavior of the female central character in several of the American films drew forth vigorous criticism. In commenting on *Mr. and Mrs. Smith*, prisoners deplored "the silly moods of Mrs. Smith," "the unnatural action presenting a husband completely dominated by his hysterical wife," "exaggerating the value of woman." The submissiveness of the father in *Shadow of a Doubt*, the "disgusting" women in *Pride and Prejudice*, and the weeping of the heroine without "deep motives" in *The More the Merrier* were also deplored by some of the prisoners, as was the lack of discipline of the children in *Shadow of a Doubt*. (*g*) By and large, the American type of farcical humor with its fast-moving and far-fetched ("silly," "crazy") developments did not have great appeal for these anti-Nazi German prisoners.

VIII

The chief conclusions to be drawn from this study are summarized below.

The 45 most popular new plays in Germany and in the United States in 1927 were analyzed for psychological content. A smaller sample from the 1909–10 period were also examined. Independent judges, from whom the difference in national origin was concealed, were used to classify the 1927 plays according to certain major categories of analysis.

The German plays are considerably more ideological, philosophical, historical, and social-minded than the American plays; the latter dwell on private problems: the difficulties of achieving love and virtue in daily life.

The German hero tends to be an individual with a quite distinct role who stands above or outside of normal society: a visionary pursuing a cause, a prince more farseeing and liberal than his subjects, a social outcast. The American hero tends to be a more ordinary person from society's midst.

The central character is less frequently a woman in the German plays than in the American, and in cases where women do have central roles in the German drama, they tend to take over masculine characteristics and masculine types of action. "Femininity" as commonly understood, feminine qualities, and feminine emotional reactions, do not get the attention in German plays that they receive in the American drama.

In the American love plots, the emphasis is upon the working out of a solution to conflicts and difficulties arising from external obstacles (e.g., parents, criminals) or from the lovers themselves (e.g., misunderstandings, immoral impulses). The path of love is precarious until some final adjustment is made. In the German plays, two individuals may be deeply united in "idyllic" love by virtue of sharing common ideals; or a physical scene or locale, charged with emotion and meaning, may provide a context for idyllic love. The German lovers, however, may be once and for all cut asunder when higher (deeper) values so dictate. The German plays do not feature the love relationship as dependent upon the solution of emotional difficulties in personal relations.

The American orientation is essentially moralistic, while the German orientation is idealistic. The American hero must struggle against immoral or antisocial tendencies in himself or in other specific individuals; such tendencies are portrayed as interfering with the normal realization of personal happiness. The German hero who stands above the masses and is pursuing an ideal goal, a blueprint for society, may have to struggle against the normal practices of society itself. The value pattern expressed in the American plays enjoins the individual to be considerate of the welfare of other individuals; at the same time he must watch out for his own welfare. The German idealistic hero, on the other hand, in order to be successful, must consider neither his own welfare nor the welfare of other specific individuals. He must consider only the fulfillment of his high aim.

Personal ambitions and personal satisfactions, which are sanctioned in the American plays, are frequently portrayed as the root obstacle in the German plays, the "materialism" against which the idealist must fight. Similarly, conventional moral standards, which in the American plays promote success and happiness, often appear in the German drama to be petty, hypocritical, mean, and confining; the German hero must frequently fight "Philistinism" as well as materialism.

Personal crimes and sins, which pose really basic problems in the American plays, are frequently excused or justified in the German plays. Society rather than the individual is pictured as responsible; or an act judged wrong by society is interpreted as good because society's judgment is petty and narrow; or a criminal act, though not approved per se, is necessitated by fate and the logic of the German idealism. We find, for example, various murders of beloved persons consciously carried out by sympathetically portrayed characters in the German plays. The American hero, placed in the same type of dilemma into which the German hero falls, might well make the same choice of action — but he does not fall into the same dilemma.

While the American plays teach the lesson that virtue has much pragmatic sanction, the lesson to be found in the German plays is that success in worldly conflicts is won through power and ruthlessness. Without power, idealism is doomed to failure. The German drama accordingly places great emphasis upon strength of character, the determined, even ruthless pursuit of long-range goals. The strong and ruthless national idealist was a German favorite of 1909–10, the humanitarian idealist overwhelmed by strong, ruthless enemies a favorite of 1927.

The good side usually triumphs in the resolution of conflicts in the American drama because some individual in a critical position changes his mind. The hero or heroine who has sinned may undergo character reform; an opposing parent, a criminal, or an estranged lover may change his attitude; or, in the last analysis, an independent tribunal of law or public opinion may be persuaded to change its opinion and recognize truth and justice. The reform of attitude or character is usually brought about through some persuasive argument or evidence, rational or irrational, such as legalistic evidence, humanitarian reasoning, a dream occasioned by eating a piece of cheese, a slap on the face, a wife's leaving her husband, sickness or injury, sudden consequences that teach a lesson. Acts of ingenuity are often the means by which the compelling evidence is marshaled. The assumption that there is a reliable fundament of good will and good sense in society making persuasion possible, that human beings can and will change provided the proper argument is brought to bear upon them — this assumption of educability and reform pervades the American drama, but is relatively lacking in the German drama. There it is assumed, on the contrary, that human beings are inflexible, uncompromising, that they are narrow in their vision, petty, and rigid in their interpretation of their status and their adherence to the canons of respectability. Even the law does not serve as an ultimate recourse, for it, too, may operate in a petty, narrow manner. It is consistent with this view of human nature and human society that conflicts are not resolved in the German drama so much through the marshaling of evidence to change attitudes, as through power techniques.

Finally, both the German and American plays express rebellion against authority: the American, against parents and others who interfere in the individual's life happiness; the German, against political superiors, classes, or society itself. The American rebels in the name of his personal right to happiness. This right is a positive value, and forces opposed to it are portrayed as immoral, evil, or at least ill-advised. There is no such right to individual happiness clearly presumed to justify rebellion against authority in the German plays. When a German rebels, he must do so not in self-interest but in the name of an ideal — a set of values which are superior to those of the authority against which he is rebelling. Each individual German rebellion thus tends to be an ideological movement.

Chapter 8

THE IMPLICATIONS OF
LEARNING THEORY FOR
SOCIAL PSYCHOLOGY

James J. Gibson
Professor of Psychology, Cornell University

THE social sciences are badly in need of a theory of human learning. They look to social psychology for the formulation of such a theory. However difficult the task may be, no other discipline is in a better position to undertake it. There are pressing problems of education, of government, and of human interaction generally which would be clarified by even a tentative scientific formulation of how man acquires his habits. What, then, should be the general characteristics of a learning theory which aims to be useful for the social sciences?

The learning with which social psychology is concerned is, of course, something broader than memorizing, or acquiring skill, or certain types of problem solving, or the learning of school subjects. These narrower forms of learning are the ones which have undergone most of the experimental analysis and are therefore the best understood. But the social psychologist conceives learning as the whole business of adjusting to human adult life. For him it means the acquisition of culture, or the ways of interacting with one's fellows, or the innumerable conscious and unconscious habits and traits of a developed personality. In present-day social psychology learning must bear the burden of accounting for attitudes, values, interests, morals, prejudices, stereotypes, ideologies, the hopes and fears of the individual, his hates and his loves, and even his ego and his superego. Learning has to be viewed as the process of socialization of the child and a prerequisite for social participation of the adult. What is required, then, is a theory of *social* learning.

When we say that the ways of a given society are learned, we mean, of course, that they are learned separately by each individual, starting in childhood. Learning is a biological function, rooted in the nervous system, and the process is connected with the prolonged dependence in the human species of the child on the parents. Although the ways of a society are common to the group, each child must learn them for himself; he will not become a civilized adult spontaneously or automatically. Far removed as it may seem, therefore, Ebbinghaus plodding over his nonsense syllables is a better guide to social learning than LeBon speculating about the group mind and the racial unconscious. For Ebbinghaus was an experimental scientist and LeBon was not. The doctrine that a culture simply perpetuates itself through the generations by analogy with a living mind is loose and dangerously misleading. Even the "laws" of imitation and suggestion, we now know, are not at all laws of learning; the imitativeness of a child requires rather than furnishes an explanation of his behavior. The nineteenth-century conception that ideas are transmitted by language from one mind to another is another theory which does not go deep enough. When a child conforms it is because he has learned a mode of conduct, not because something called an idea has been inserted into his head. Freud saw the essential problem: "What ways and means," he asked, "does a generation use to transfer its psychic states to the next generation?" This was an inquiry about what we would call today the learning process in children. Like the learning of nonsense syllables and mazes, the critical process takes place inside the single individual.

Freud's question, of course, was also an inquiry about the behavior of parents. The point is important, because here we see a fundamental requirement for any theory of social learning: Unlike a theory for nonsense syllables and mazes, it must take account of social interaction — the "ways and means" of adults dealing with children — and therefore must inevitably refer to behavior *outside* of the single individual. Important as it is to avoid mystification about the group mind and valuable as it is to localize learning within the child, the social psychologist must begin his analysis of learning not with the classical problem situation but with the parent-child situation. This will be the principal thesis and also the main difficulty of the discussion which is to follow.

The main lines of scientific thought on which the social psychologist can draw for his theory of learning are (1) the conceptions of the Gestalt theorists, (2) the system of psychoanalysis, and (3) the contemporary theories of learning derived from laboratory evidence. There is no reason why he should not borrow concepts from any of these sources if they fit the problems of socialization, personality development, and cultural change. It might be argued that none of these lines of scientific thought is yet ready for application to such complex social problems. But students of these problems cannot sit and wait. If the social psychologist does not formulate a theory of learning, the cultural anthropologist will have to do so — and also the psychiatrist, the clinician, the educator, and the student of child development. Collaborative efforts in this direction have already appeared by Mowrer and Kluckhohn,[1] Miller and Dollard,[2] and a committee of the National Society for the Study of Education.[3] The evidence for a theory of learning is not yet complete for any systematic approach, but it is by no means negligible and it points clearly in certain directions.

Among these three approaches, the concepts of Lewin and the Gestalt theorists are of least value, I suggest, for the

[1] Mowrer, O. H., and Kluckhohn, C. Dynamic theory of personality. In *Personality and the behavior disorders.* New York: Ronald, 1944. Chap. 3.

[2] Miller, N. E., and Dollard, J. *Social learning and imitation.* New Haven: Yale Univ. Press, 1941.

[3] National Society for the Study of Education, *Forty-first Yearbook. Part II, The psychology of learning.* Chicago: Univ. of Chicago Press, 1942.

particular task at hand, not because of their validity but because of their applicability. They apply to the child's appre-
hension of his situation rather than to his habits; they are
successful in "catching upon the wing the flying vectors of
immediate motivation"[4] but not in tracing the *development*
of the child's motives. Concepts borrowed or adapted from
Freud, however, are indispensable for a theory of social
learning because no psychologist has understood the role of
the parents in forming the habits of the child as clearly as he.
Concepts taken from the contemporary theories of learning
— those of Hull, Thorndike, Tolman, Guthrie, and Skinner —
should be most useful of all since they are founded on experimental evidence and have been developed under the stimulus of searching scientific criticism. These general theories
have reached such a level that they ought to be put to the
test of fitting facts other than those from which they were
derived — the facts of social learning.

The difficulty is that the experimentally founded theories
— Hull's, for instance — do *not* fit the facts of social learning
in one important respect. As now formulated, they do not
account for the astonishing prevalence of moral behavior
among human adults. Having a high regard for biological
facts, as these theories do, the relation of learning to need
satisfaction tends to be their central emphasis, and having
animal behavior as a main source of experimental data their
orientation is toward animal learning. This point is so
important that we ought to consider it at some length. It
is one reason, I think, why Allport has recently asserted that
need satisfaction is if only minor importance in human
learning as compared with the "structure of the ego."[5]

[4] Rice, P. B. The ego and the law of effect. *Psychol. Rev.*, 1946,
53:307–319.

[5] Allport, G. W. The ego in contemporary psychology. *Psychol. Rev.*,
1943, 50:451–478.

Allport, G. W. Effect: a secondary principle of learning. *Psychol.
Rev.*, 1946, 53:335–347.

It is perfectly true that human adults are unlike animals. Human adults, for example, do not simply eat when they are hungry; they even go so far as to get hungry by the clock. Human adults do not, when hungry, appropriate and eat food when they see it; they go through roundabout and inexpedient acts such as purchase. Human adults do not often, when sexually excited, approach the nearest visible female or male; the approach tends to be highly roundabout and is usually stereotyped. It is easy to multiply examples: Among us, men do not, when wet by rain, go to the nearest house for shelter; and grownups, when going from here to there, do not take the direct route but walk only on sidewalks and streets. Moreover, people in groups do not go to sleep when they are sleepy, they do not take off their shoes when their feet are pinched, and they do not take off their clothes when they are hot. Academic social psychology flourishes on such classroom insights as these, and the debunking of taboos is the stock in trade of many a social science teacher.

Let us, however, take this biologically ridiculous behavior of man quite seriously. How is it to be accounted for? Behavior of this sort is not predictable from the assumption that habit formation is governed simply by the satisfaction of biological drives, or need reduction. If the satisfying or annoying outcome of behavior *for an isolated animal* were the sole basis for the reinforcement of action, one could never account for the above kinds of learning. The child, however, is not isolated. Its habit formation is governed not only by need satisfaction but by what we call training, or, fundamentally, by punishment and reward. These latter reinforcing agents are usually lumped together with need satisfaction in most discussions of the law of effect, but let it be noted that punishments and rewards are necessarily social acts. They are administered by a parent or a trainer; they emanate from another organism who is always a part of the stimulus situation of the learner, except in those special experimental conditions when the learner is shut up in a box or a maze. Merely to assume that a parent is a stimulus object like any other, or that the social situation is a more complex maze situation, is to lose sight of the unique function of *the other organism* as a reinforcing agent. The problem of accounting for secondary reinforcement and acquired motives in contemporary learning theory needs reorientation toward this unique function.

Now, isolated animals and children when they are left to themselves *do* appear to learn by the simple rule of need satisfaction. It accounts for the animal experiments, and it accounts for much of the behavior of children — that behavior which Freud ascribed to the "pleasure principle." Current discussions of the law of effect and the principle of reinforcement in learning[6] would be clarified, I think, if the point should be insisted upon that punishment and reward imply social reinforcement whereas drive satisfaction may consist of nonsocial or merely environmental reinforcement. The learning situations which have been devised for animals are of the latter type, and to speak of the animal as receiving a food *reward* or being administered *punishment* by electric shock is only to encourage confusion.

I suggest that the social psychologist ought to distinguish at the outset between habits induced by the material environment and habits induced by social training. If the distinction is granted we can describe both the inhibitory or roundabout actions of human adults, and the immediately satisfying and direct actions of animals and children, as *learned* — but learned with a difference. The former we may call *proper* learning and the latter *expedient* learning. When a child learns to get a cookie only by first passing

[6] For example *cf.* Mowrer, O. H. The law of effect and ego psychology. *Psychol. Rev.*, 1946, 53:321–334.

Allport, G. W. Effect: a secondary principle of learning. *Ibid.*, 335–347.

the plate politely, this is proper behavior; when he snatches it (or when a rat learns to get a food pellet by pressing a bar), this is expedient behavior. The reinforcing of expedient acts is theoretically straightforward, as Hull has demonstrated.[7] It is the reinforcing of proper acts which presents theoretical difficulties and which, in the fully developed forms of proper behavior, makes a hedonistic theory inapplicable and makes the emphasis on learning as a purely intellectual function appear to best advantage.

The terms *expedient* and *proper* admittedly have a moral flavor. They are terms borrowed from the vernacular, as Skinner puts it,[8] which are to be avoided in scientific psychology because they introduce unexamined conceptual schemes or assumptions. For these terms, however, we propose to employ the implicit meanings. The moral flavor is present because we undertake to deal with moral behavior at the start. Social learning is inevitably moral, in an elementary sense of the term, and it is probably a mistake first to construct a behavior theory without reference to social interaction, and then to attach it only at the end. Expedient ways of action are those reinforced by effects confined to the material environment; and they are defined in inverse terms of the effort and time (and possibly pain) involved in the action. Proper ways of action are those reinforced by effects on the behavior of other individuals (reward and punishment, to begin with) and are defined in terms of the habits of parents determining their acts of approval or disapproval, or cultural expectations. Expedient behavior is that which satisfies biological drives. Proper behavior is that which conforms to customs and mores.

We can now observe that not *all* acts reinforced by social

[7] Hull, C. L. *Principles of behavior.* New York: Appleton-Century-Crofts, 1943.

[8] Skinner, B. F. *The behavior of organisms.* New York: Appleton-Century-Crofts, 1938.

training are inhibitory or roundabout. Much of our socially patterned behavior is directly need satisfying, or, as we now may say, expedient as well as proper. Although human adults do not eat when they see food, they do make ingenious customary arrangements to keep it close at hand. Although they do not walk "cross-lots," they use vehicles which will travel the roundabout way of the streets with even less time and effort. They may not take off their clothes when hot, but they do have clothes for when it is cold. Civilization consists of techniques as well as taboos — a fact which Freud and the psychoanalysts have never fully realized. "The best way" in a problem situation involving a choice of behavior routes may refer to a technical tradition as well as to a moral tradition. The use of fire, shoes, vehicles, and laborsaving machines, along with all the other expediting tricks that men have invented, are technical traditions. Habits of this kind should in theory be readily learned and easily modified since the reinforcing effect of training and that of simple need reduction are conjoined. Habits which are proper but inexpedient, or improper but expedient, should in theory be subject to habit interference and would be expected to constitute the important problems for a theory of social learning. The point to be noted, however, is that these types of behavior are not *necessarily* in conflict.

The outcome of these first considerations is the conclusion that a theory of social learning should look upon the process as intraorganic but as having an essential relation to interorganic situations. It should be rooted in the motivation of an organism but nevertheless oriented toward the social patterning of the individual's acts.

The Desirable Features of a Theory for Social Psychology

It might be useful to attempt a list of the main features which a theory of social learning should have. At least the *kind* of postulates and terms for a theory could be indicated for purposes of discussion. The first feature is the assumption that learning is a biological function of the organism. In this respect the theory would resemble both Hull's system of behavior and that of an earlier theorist, E. B. Holt, whose *Animal Drive and the Learning Process*[9] has much in common with it. This fundamental premise, to give a negative illustration, would be incompatible with Allport's emphasis that learning is a function not of the *organism* but of the *person.*[10] These two terms are partly a matter of choice, no doubt, but there is a danger that Allport's term will be interpreted to mean that what learns is some kind of a learner within the organism. Men are living animals. They are organisms first and self-conscious persons second.

The second feature we might agree upon is that, although the theory should begin with drives and the principle of need reduction, it should by no means end there. It must account first for the behavior of the child, but it should proceed to account next for the socialized behavior of adults, and the postulates of the theory ought to be formulated with this aim in view. If behavior is inescapably related to the mores, the assumptions about human reinforcing agents should be explicit.

Third, and here we introduce a new issue, the theory should reject the assumptions which underlie the whole doctrine of "original" human nature. One such assumption is Thorndike's opinion that the child is equipped with a set of unmodifiable stimulus-response connections. Another is the older view that motives or instincts remain unchanged throughout life and that the veneer of culture can be peeled off to reveal them. Freud's opposition between the superego

[9] Holt, E. B. *Animal drive and the learning process.* New York: Holt, 1931.

[10] Allport, G. W. The ego in contemporary psychology. *Psychol. Rev.,* 1943, 50:451–478.

and the id implies the same thing. A modern equivalent is the view that the learning process is distinct and separable from the maturation process. All these presuppose a fixed foundation of motivation and behavior on which learning is superimposed. But the chief lesson of modern anthropology is that not only men's behavior but also their motives are socially patterned. The drives appear to be transformed in the learning process and new motives to emerge. The behavior which is supposed to constitute culture is not a separate kind which is distinguishable from "natural" or "original" behavior, the one being learned and the other innate. Instead we suggest that *all* behavior is both socially patterned and individually acquired. What gets learned tends to be *both* socially permissible and individually workable, or *both* proper and expedient. Although the reinforcing tendencies defined by what we have called propriety and expediency may work in opposition, this conflict does not ordinarily yield two separate systems of habits.

Fourth, the theory should avoid entanglements with such problems as whether the environment is constituted of isolated stimuli, and whether behavior is composed of elementary responses. The perception of objects and space has been sufficiently dealt with by Koffka;[11] and the fact of molar behavior has been so persuasively argued by Tolman [12] that the social psychologist would do well simply to take them as given. He should freely use terms such as *objects,* or *events,* instead of *stimuli,* and should substitute *acts* for *responses.* (Even though the problems of perceptual constancy and of equivalent responses are not yet solved, they are outside the scope of social psychology since they have to do primarily with the relation between the organism and the material en-

[11] Koffka, K. *Principles of Gestalt psychology.* New York: Harcourt Brace, 1927.

[12] Tolman, E. C. *Purposive behavior in animals and men.* New York: Appleton-Century-Crofts, 1932.

vironment.) He must also be free to talk about the *meaning* of objects and events. Although men of different cultures sense the material world in about the same way, the world of symbols and values, friends and enemies, of institutions and groups, is dependent on learning, and this learning conforms to perceptual customs. Whether this cognitive learning is subject to the principle of reinforcement seems to be debatable, but it is in any case inseparable from language and social interaction and is therefore a branch of the theory of social learning. The acquisition of meaning can be studied with emphasis on a hypothetical process of sensory organization or with emphasis on a hypothetical process of sign-learning. The verbal learning experiment and the conditioning experiment have been the chief sources of experimental data for this study, but although a great deal of evidence has been gathered, the theoretical background for meaning and concept formation is not yet clear. The influence of social norms on the perceptions and "values" of the individual has been profusely demonstrated by experiment, however, and although these studies are actually observations rather than true systematic experiments, there is a tendency among social psychologists to see in them the prototype of all social learning. Meaning, however, cannot be the *starting point* for the kind of theory we require. Even if such a theory of socially determined judgments were fully worked out, would it be a substitute for a theory of socially determined conduct? It can account for stereotypes, errors of observation, misunderstandings among men of different traditions, and differences between *your* phenomenal world and *mine*, but it has no explanation for veridical perception and it fails to connect meaning with adaptive behavior.

Fifth, a treatment of social learning should employ the terms of behavior theory without subscribing to the notion that they are the only valid terms for psychology. Terms referring to action rather than to perception are usually preferable in describing the learning of children, for example. Up to the point where behavior terms become unwieldy or begin to fail altogether, they are usually more precise and more definable than perceptual terms. Ultimately the two may prove to be equally valid, and even mutually translatable, but the terminology of social perception at present is subject to rapidly changing fashions. An example is the term "frame of reference," which is being used with something like abandon. For Koffka it meant the implicit axes of visual space perception — essentially what it means in geometry. [13] For Sherif, as a result of his famous spot-of-light experiment, it meant first a norm or standard on a scale of judgment, and second a miniature perceptual custom.[14] For some psychologists, however, it apparently can mean any attitude whatever, such as the habit of wearing clothes.

Sixth, a theory of social learning should try to formulate predictions about whatever it is that is called the ego. In this respect the theory would conform to the ideas of Allport, who has recently argued that it is high time to bring the ego back into psychology.[15] But Allport appears to be convinced that the interests or motives which comprise the ego have far more effect on learning that has any principle of biological reinforcement or any variant of the law of effect.[16] The ego-motives are, he says, *psychogenic;* the primary determinant of learning is the existing pattern of the personality which tends to maintain itself. A statement of this sort could hardly be made about the child, and it would appear that Allport is not thinking of a theory of social learning but that he has his eye fixed on the adult personality of the single

[13] Koffka, *op. cit.*

[14] Sherif, M. *The psychology of social norms.* New York: Harper, 1936.

[15] Allport, The ego in contemporary psychology, *loc. cit.*

[16] Allport, Effect: a secondary principle of learning, *loc. cit.*

individual with all its fascinating complexity of structure. Both Rice [17] and Mowrer [18] have undertaken to argue the point with Allport and to assert that so far from the ego-motives being the primary determinants of learning, it is the other way around: learning accounts for the attitudes and interests which compose the ego. This is the position which I would accept; and would we not agree that it is the position which any genetic theory of social learning must adopt?

As a first step the theory should analyze and define the complex of what Allport calls ego-involved behavior. There exist observations of such behavior in children, and a few semiexperimental studies. Their evidence suggests that self-assertion is a hierarchy of habits and attitudes. The simple competitive situation should provide an opportunity for true experiments when the needed theoretical scheme is constructed. If two-year-old children pay no attention to a competitor but four-year-olds do, the likeliest hypothesis is that the latter have begun to learn competitive habits. Are these generalized or specific, and is the reinforcing agent the satisfaction of possessing or consuming the goal object or is it from the outset a social reward? The competitive situation can be defined in theoretical terms. The simplest is a two-child problem situation, involving reciprocal alternatives of satisfaction or frustration. What, then, can be predicted from these terms about the learning which each child will undergo when satisfied and when frustrated? Does the status of having-an-object-which-another-child-wants-but-does-not-have come to be valued independently of any pre-existing value of the object itself? This would be at least the type of procedure needed.

When experimental evidence about rivalry and self-assertion accumulates it can be compared with the data of Piaget

[17] Rice, *op. cit.*

[18] Mowrer, *op. cit.*

and the theory of Mead and others regarding the ways in which the child's ego becomes differentiated *in experience*.[19] The ego conceived as an organized set of perceptions, meanings, and values is presumably just as analyzable as it is when conceived as a pattern of habits, although the analysis may give more trouble. Perhaps the ego is actually a number of different experiences with little in common except the name. Although it is time to bring back the ego to psychology, it needs to be analyzed rather than reinstated to the position it occupied in mental philosophy, as Allport is the first to admit.[20]

THE FUNDAMENTAL PATTERN OF MORAL BEHAVIOR

We have proposed six requirements to be met by a theory of the social learning process. Some of these requirements may appear to be contradictory. The theorist never knows until he tries, however, whether or not a contradiction can be resolved. The most fundamental of all, perhaps, is the one with which we started — the demand that our theory accept need satisfaction as the reinforcing mechanism of human learning and that it then proceed to account for moral behavior as learned. If this is a paradox for social psychology, some comfort may be taken in remembering that it has also long been a paradox for ethics. Many students of ethics have found no explanation of human morality short of a supernatural one, and perhaps this is the reason why social psychologists are wary of the term and are disinclined to attack the problem. But the problem is implicit in any learning theory when it is applied to concrete human behavior. The law of effect in its original form implies a crude hedonism. If any part of human behavior is not consistent

[19] Sherif, M., and Cantril, H. *The psychology of ego-involvements.* New York: Wiley, 1947.

[20] Allport, The ego in contemporary psychology, *loc. cit.*

with hedonism the law of effect has to be either modified or supplemented. The former is the course which Thorndike himself has chosen in his recent emphasis on the "confirming reaction." [21] But the latter is equally possible and perhaps preferable for social psychology.

The possibility of accounting for moral behavior as learned, starting with need reduction as the primary reinforcing mechanism, is suggested by the following theoretical stages of development. It should be emphasized that the stages are intended to be logical rather than chronological. At first the child learns expedient ways of satisfying his needs, and these are reinforced by the simplest forms of gratification. To some extent this process continues throughout life, so long as the expedient ways do not result in punishment or conflict with other habits which develop later. This is trial-and-error, or instrumental, learning.

Next, the child encounters the administered punishments and rewards of the parent which reinforce a set of proper ways and frequently require inexpedient behavior (but sometimes, at least, permit even more expedient ways in the form of skills than the child would ever have learned by himself). The overt punishments and rewards can give way to signs of approval and disapproval in so far as the child has learned the signs. This process also continues throughout life, with other individuals, agencies, and even abstract symbols substituting for the parent. The mere *anticipation* of punishment or reward may have a reinforcing effect on the proper way if occasional reinforcements are administered. Such learning is complex, and it involves anxiety, conflict, and occasional frustration. The symptoms of it are manifold and familiar. Its effect is to produce in the child (and in the

[21]Thorndike, E. L. A theory of the action of the after-effects of a connection upon it. *Psychol. Rev.*, 1933, 40:434–439.

Thorndike, E. L. *The psychology of wants, interests, and attitudes.* New York: Teach. Coll. Bur. Pub., 1935.

adult) a profound interest in the behavior of other individuals and a strong complex of motives to communicate, to modify their behavior, and to try, in the words of Dale Carnegie, to win friends and influence people. So far, we may note, the reinforcement process is similar to that observed in the animal-learning experiments.

A third stage occurs when the child begins to have a need for punishment after a bit of wrongdoing and a genuine appetite for approval after proper behavior. This develops into the capacity for self-punishment, or guilt feeling, and for self-approbation, or feelings of self-satisfaction. How such development occurs is not known, but the clue to it may be that the reinforcement process no longer needs to be initiated by another person but can be aroused by a concept of, or an attitude toward, one's own act. Freud's description of this step in development is a figurative one. He postulates an entity called the superego or conscience and accounts for it by supposing that the "image" of the parent, who prohibits and punishes but also commands and rewards, is incorporated into the personality. The child swallows the parent and thereby introjects the culture. This lively dramatization of ill-identified psychological processes is easier to criticize than it is to supplant. The mechanism of "internal" reinforcement needs to be studied experimentally in children. For there can be no doubt but that some persons at least need no longer be overtly punished or rewarded after childhood in order for their conduct to remain proper although inexpedient. Habit formation of this sort accounts for a great deal of law-abiding, conforming, right-thinking, and conventionally moral conduct of ordinary human beings. Except for the temptations to expedient behavior in driving and parking automobiles, and a few other situations where the required proper behavior is equally arbitrary, a great many citizens behave themselves with no overt reinforcements whatever.

A fourth stage begins when the child first performs an act which yields a primary satisfaction *only* to someone else — usually the parent. Such acts are seldom inexpedient ones at the outset and never ones which are actually painful or self-depriving. They are reinforced at first by reward and approval, but that is not the point. Some of them probably are, or come to be, reinforced by a purely vicarious pleasure in the satisfaction of the other individual, and the significant fact is that this seems to occur only when the child "puts himself in the place of" the other individual. This latter mechanism, whatever its explanation may be, is of the very first importance for social psychology and social learning. It is, of course, what Freud called ego-identification. It is closely related to what social psychologists have called the reaction of sympathy and to the mechanism which underlies the most significant kind of imitation. This projection of the ego will not be understood until we know more about the complex of problems labeled ego-development. But the suggestion is that the need satisfaction of another person can be *substituted,* as it were, for the need satisfaction of the learner himself in the reinforcement process if this projection of the ego has taken place. Such behavior is properly called ethical or altruistic. The traditional explanation of it has been in terms of purely intellectual processes, assuming it to be based on rational comprehension and, in fact, to appear only at the "age of reason." But one does not have to assume that a six-year-old child gets an occasional flash of insight into the categorical imperative in order to explain his generous impulses. He is more likely to be identifying himself with the beneficiary of his act. Such behavior seems to occur earlier than reasoned altruistic behavior and is possibly fundamental to it.

The mechanism of ego-identification, or something like it, increases in scope during social development and comes to be applied not only to an increasing circle of individuals but also to groups of individuals: family, community, profession, class, nation — even the human species as a whole. All the evidence about social distance, sympathy, and group membership points in this direction. If we assume that a vicarious satisfaction can be a reinforcing process, just as a primary satisfaction is, when the learner has identified himself with a group, we shall begin to understand problems of great importance for the applied social sciences. The nature of the cooperating group and the secondary satisfaction which individuals obtain by participating in it are one outstanding question. The abstract question of whether and how a group can regulate the behavior of its members to their "mutual benefit" is another. The concept of mutual benefit is an old one in political and economic theory; laws have been written on the basis of one or another interpretation of it, and conflicting political ideologies differ over its meaning. The mores of a group might be accounted for by assuming that the inexpedient performances required of children got the status of propriety because they made the behavior of *others* expedient. But this is not what is meant by mutual benefit. The conception is that there are some ways of behavior which are more than proper or moral — ways which are expedient for *all* members of the group and which resolve the conflict between expedient and proper alternatives. Such ways of behavior involve novel types of social interaction and unquestionably have to be learned. They are techniques of social interaction analogous to the highly expedient techniques of what is called material culture. The study of them is at once ethics and social technology, and there is no need to believe that these disciplines must necessarily conflict.

The requirements and responsibilities of a theory of social learning may seem overwhelming to the habitual experimenter, and the theory demanded may appear much too grandiose. Scientists, he will object, should proceed step by step, and with caution. But this, I assert, is a misplaced emphasis. The stepwise and careful procedure applies to the scientist's methods, not to the scope and range of his theories or to the plans which he may lay out for them. Social psychology has no choice but to make grandiose plans. They may or may not come to fulfillment, but it is worth trying.

Chapter 9

SOCIAL PSYCHOLOGY AND
THE ATOMIC BOMB:
A ROUND-TABLE DISCUSSION

Members of the Symposium
and
Leo Szilard
Professor of Biophysics, University of Chicago

All the speakers at the symposium participated in the following discussion, in addition to Mr. Szilard, who was active in the wartime research which produced the atomic bomb, and Dr. James G. Miller. Mr. Marquis was chairman.

MR. MARQUIS: When we were planning this round table the group suggested that I should start by pointing out that scientists traditionally have freedom to pick the problems they're going to work on, that it has always been the prerogative of a physicist to choose that problem within that branch of physics on which he thinks his work will be productive, and that this has led to beneficial results in the development of science. Even industrial laboratories, where they're perfectly sure what they want in the end, have found that it pays to let scientists work on the problems that they think will turn out to be productive. Well, we weren't so fortunate tonight. We didn't pick this problem. But we do recognize that there comes a time when scientists can't choose, if the problems are created by forces outside science. Then scientists must contribute what they can to the solution of those problems. This is by way of apology and explanation.

Now, there's one man here tonight who by virtue of circumstances has thought about the atomic bomb longer than any of the rest of us. While we do not expect him to reveal any secrets, I should like to ask Mr. Szilard if he would tell us the results of his thinking about the psychological issues that are created by the atomic bomb.

MR. SZILARD: A newspaperman has summed up these effects in one single sentence. He said, "The effect of the atomic bomb which was dropped on Hiroshima seems to vary with the distance." It fell on the Japanese and it got the Americans excited. This is quite understandable, of course. The Japanese, having lost the war, live now in hope, and we, having won the war, live in fear. As long as the major weapons of the war consisted of guns, tanks, and airplanes, we could outproduce all other countries in these weapons, and we could not fail ultimately to win any war. Moreover, we could be confident that any war in which we might get involved would be fought on someone else's territory. This will no longer be true ten or fifteen years from now. Other countries as well as ourselves will have large stock piles of atomic bombs. The only protection against a large-scale attack by such bombs would consist in the defense of our cities, and we should begin to defend them, on a large scale, ten years prior to the outbreak of the next war. The only real safeguard against the atomic bomb is, of course, to have no war in which it would be used. How to bring this about is not for a physicist to say, and I'm handing this problem, therefore, to the psychologists who are here present. But speaking not as a physicist, but merely as a human being, I would propose as a first step that the message of the Bible be amended to read, "He who lives by the bomb, shall perish by the bomb." In the long run no nation can violate the command of the Bible without acquiring a bad conscience. When John Hersey wrote "Hiroshima," an entire number of *The New Yorker* was devoted to it, and there was an immediate and extraordinary public response to this bit of writing here in America. By contrast, Hersey's "Hiroshima" brought little public reaction in England and I am told that large stocks of copies remain unsold in the British bookstores. The difference in American and British reactions to "Hiroshima" seems to indicate that we feel very much responsible for the bombing of Hiroshima, while the British do not.

So far I have touched upon two points: fear of what the defense position of the nation may be some ten years hence, and a bad conscience as a result of what we have done when we set the precedent of using the atomic bomb for purposes of destruction. It seems to me that the combination of fear and bad conscience is a particularly dangerous combination.

There is also another effect of the bomb which can be called overconfidence. Because we have large stock piles of bombs and Russia has not so many, most people believe that if it came to a war with Russia in the next few years, we would not fail to win. We would knock out much of Russia's production capacity right at the start of the war and would follow this up by an invasion of Europe that would ultimately win the war for us. This being the case, we are inclined to feel that it is unforgivable on the part of Russia to be so unyielding and thereby to try our patience and lead us into temptation. If you read Mr. Byrnes's book, *Speaking Frankly*, you will find in it, described in detail, the first major negotiations with Russia which followed the bombing of Hiroshima. This was a conference of foreign ministers, held in London in September of 1945, one month after Hiroshima. This conference was stalemated from its very beginning. Mr. Byrnes explains that at first he attributed this failure to our reluctance to agree to some of Russia's aspirations. Much later, so he said, he came to the conclusion that he was all wrong and that the annoying acts of the Russians at London arose from their dissatisfaction with our handling of the Japanese issue. The atomic bomb was not discussed at London at all, nor does Mr. Byrnes make any reference to it in connection with the difficulties which he encountered in London in his negotiations. But I would like tentatively to offer to you a further explanation for the total failure of the London conference. My theory depends on the influence exerted by the bomb on the minds of those who negotiated in London on behalf of the United States. They could not help but be impressed by the power which the possession of the atomic bomb seemed to give to the United States at that juncture. I would go further to venture the hypothesis that the bomb had cast its shadow ahead

of it and was responsible for some of the difficulties which
had arisen at Potsdam in July, 1945. The belief of some of
our statesmen and above all the general belief of the American public that because we have possession of the bomb we
are at present all-powerful and invincible is possibly the most
important single effect exerted by the atomic bomb upon
world events.

Mr. Marquis: Mr. Szilard, did I understand you to say
that the only defense against the atom bomb would be the
prevention of war?

Mr. Szilard: Yes, I said so.

Mr. Marquis: Thus, by one stroke, changing the problem
from one of physics to one of social psychology. Well, perhaps you're right. The prevention of war is, I suppose, a
matter of convictions and beliefs. It is in part a moral problem, and I suppose that social psychology could contribute,
therefore, by study of the values and the ideas of people
in an attempt to discover which values are strongest in their
opposing war, and also what would be the most effective
ways to strengthen and propagate those values. But it
isn't only a moral question. The world does contain, I'm
sure we all believe, a preponderance of men of good will, and
I'm certain that if a public opinion poll were taken throughout the world we would find that more than a majority are
in favor of peace. But nevertheless, we seem to be moving
in the direction of greater and greater conflict and the likelihood of renewed war. Now you pointed out, Mr. Szilard,
that the bomb also has an effect on attitudes which might
lead to war. Well, suppose we take the present international
negotiations as an example. The existence of the atomic
bomb, as you said, creates a clear possibility of war — a war
in which our country would be involved as directly and immediately as any other country; that is, it will be fought in
our country as well as in others. Now, the possibility of
war places a responsibility and obligation on our leaders to

secure certain advantages that would be necessary in the event of war. When they seek to secure these advantages, resentment and counterreaction are created on the part of other countries, which in turn enhance our recognition of the possibility of war and the necessity of developing further advantages. It seems that we get caught in a vicious circle in which one event leads to steps toward war, which lead to similar steps in other countries, and so on. What I'm trying to get at is that this vicious circle of events may take place even though the people are of good will and desire peace and may get to a point where it is impossible to break out of the circular regress, and then things lead inexorably to armed conflict. Now this same kind of circle of attitudes and expectations can exist within our country. That is, public opinion in our country exerts influences and checks upon the actions of our governmental leaders. They, in turn, if they act, have an effect upon public opinion. For example, the Truman doctrine, which was a statement that we would move into Greece and Turkey, immediately set the general public in this country to contemplating the possibility of war. Then that reaction strengthens the government in its next step in that direction and in part forces it, and when that step is taken it again changes public opinion, so that we have the possibility of a vicious circle. It may be that there are technical ways of studying this and getting at measures by which one could control or break a circle which leads to a point where armed conflict is inevitable.

This analysis of the problem puts it in a social psychological setting. I think we might turn to ask what social psychology, with its concepts and methods, could say about such a problem. There are, of course, different ways in which such a problem could be attacked. There will be need for immediate approaches involving the knowledge that we already have or whatever can be accomplished in research in a few years; then there can be medium-range and long-range work. We hope that the immediate steps we take will hold off conflict and so make long-range studies possible. I think tonight we might concentrate on some of the more immediate and direct applications of social psychology to this problem. In it the important variables are the convictions, attitudes, and expectations of peoples and of their leaders, imbedded in their ideologies, their customs, and their cultures. What can social psychology contribute to such a problem? This is open for discussion, gentlemen.

MR. CARTWRIGHT: It seems to me that how the problem is formulated, its determinants, and how it gets involved in these vicious circles we are talking about may be viewed as a matter of public opinion. Social scientists have developed, in the past ten years or so, research techniques to learn a great deal about public opinion. There are many research organizations in existence today making regular studies of public opinion. Some of them are well known and publicized, such as the Gallup poll, the Roper poll, and the National Opinion Research Center. Others are not so well publicized but are doing useful work also — the Survey Research Center of the University of Michigan, and others. As a result of these studies we know some things about public reactions to the atomic bomb. Surveys were in existence before the bomb was made, and special research on reactions to the atomic bomb has been carried out since then. Perhaps the most intensive study of this sort was conducted about the time of the Bikini test, to get some measures of the effect of that event upon public opinion. In order to show what research has taught us about the way people are reacting to the fact of the atomic bomb, I'll refer briefly to some of the findings of that study.

First, it was found that the fact of the atomic bomb was well known throughout the entire population. It may seem obvious to us that everyone would know it, but you'd be surprised how many people have never heard of the United

Nations, for example.   This survey found that people who had never heard of the United Nations nonetheless had heard about the atomic bomb.   Hardly anyone can be found who hasn't heard about it.   Now, popular concepts of what the bomb is and what it can do vary tremendously throughout the population.   Some of them are very primitive, almost magical, being involved in sectarian views of the nature of the world, theological considerations, and so on, but everyone who knows anything about it is aware that it is extremely destructive.   Whatever else they think about it, they're fully aware that it's a destructive force.   As a matter of fact, it's interesting how many people before the Bikini test, in describing what they thought would happen there, would talk about the island disappearing and give quite fantastic accounts of its destructiveness.   But despite this, the results seem quite paradoxical, because, as far as we can determine, the American public is not particularly emotionally distressed by the bomb.   The majority appear to have found a way of pushing the bomb out of consciousness or at least putting it into the back of their minds.   Many psychological mechanisms for doing this have been discovered.   For example, many people argue that the creative genius that invented the atomic bomb can invent a defense against it, so there's nothing to worry about.   Some feel confident that if we have the bomb no other country would dare provoke war against us, so we're safe.   Others are willing to admit the worst, but seek at least superficial refuge in a fatalistic acceptance of it.   They say, "Well, everybody's got to die sometime, so I don't care whether it's the atomic bomb or something else that ends my life.   If it hits me I'll never know it."   Others feel that responsibility for dealing with the problem rests entirely with the authorities.   "There's nothing I can do about it, so why should I worry?"   And so on. These are mechanisms that people have employed to escape worry.

MR. MARQUIS: Would this mean, then, that we have no evidence that the atomic bomb is a strong force leading people to take drastic actions for peace? Some of us hoped once, I know, that it would be so frightening that men would be willing to sacrifice almost anything, even national sovereignty, for peace.

MR. CARTWRIGHT: Well, I'm afraid that the evidence we have so far is that the fact of the atomic bomb has not worked as many thought it might. I think people have pushed it away from their thinking and have tried to avoid it. That doesn't mean it isn't having an effect upon their thinking. I think it means that the processes are not conscious and rational. They are more likely to be emotional and I think we have evidence of greater tendency to hysteria. Perhaps all the flying-saucer incidents were somehow related to this.

DR. MILLER: I wonder if that isn't an important consideration in evaluating findings from public opinion polls? In general, polls discover only conscious attitudes, and you have to get other types of evidence about the unconscious mechanisms which, if there's any basis to psychoanalytic theory, are frequently more potent than the conscious ones. Consider, for example, the evidence that Dr. Szilard mentioned about the popularity of the article "Hiroshima" here and in England. One might suspect that that would indicate that there was more unconscious anxiety and guilt about this problem in America than in England, even though public opinion polls might not demonstrate this.

MR. CARTWRIGHT: It would be an unwarranted conclusion to say that we can jump immediately from an answer to some issue given in a public opinion poll to certainty about what is going to happen. Nonetheless, the pressures exerted on our public leaders, voting in elections, and such political acts occur at a manifest level and not an unconscious one, whatever the more fundamental determinants may be.

I wonder, at this point, if it wouldn't be interesting to look a bit into what some of these attitudes are toward a problem like who should know the secrets of the bomb and control its manufacture and use. Let me just read off a list of assertions that more than half of the population endorsed when these specific issues were put to them: Seventy-five per cent of the people hold a belief that the United States should retain control of the bomb, rather than letting the United Nations have control of it. Seventy per cent believe that the United States should continue making bombs, at least temporarily. Coupled with a readiness to try to work out some form of international regulation that would prevent any nation, including the United States, from using the bomb, they still have these other beliefs: that we should not give the secrets away now, and that we should continue manufacturing the bomb. There is great doubt among the majority of the population that international control is likely to be successful.

Now, one of the underlying attitudes that seem to determine a lot of these specific attitudes about what should be done with the bomb, I think, is our view of our own nation as being essentially altruistic and humanitarian. There's a strong conviction that as long as the bomb is in our hands, the world is safe. We would not use it for aggression, and we cannot see why any other country is particularly disturbed about our having it. That, I think, is one of the more fundamental points of view that determine thinking about these specific issues as they come up.

Well, that gets us into the whole matter of relations among nations, and I think one or two points there are important. Thinking now about the atomic bomb is oriented almost entirely within the context of our relations with Russia. The American people are distrustful of Russia at present. Russia is viewed as uncooperative, stubborn, negativistic, always vetoing everything. She is viewed as being concerned with political expansion. She threatens the internal stability of other nations. So we get into the problem of communism in this country. I believe that in public thinking the two issues have now got tied up so closely that we have a different situation in dealing with Russia and the atomic bomb than we would have with any other country. Immediately the bomb is tied up with domestic conflicts and internal difficulties. Where does the hope of the American people lie? They are strongly behind the idea of the United Nations. They hope that the United Nations can do something to help solve this problem. They believe we should help make the United Nations strong. But there are some very disturbing things here. Confidence in the United Nations is sagging. In May of 1946, 37 per cent of the public said they were dissatisfied with the way the United Nations was going, and by September, 1947, that had risen to 51 per cent. There's a marked shift, and if the trend continues it will result in a great skepticism about the United Nations. Dissatisfaction with the progress of international relations is connected closely with belief in the inevitability of war. A recent survey contained the question: "Do you think there will or will not be another war within the next ten years?" Fifty-three per cent thought there would be; 36 per cent thought not; and 11 per cent ventured no opinion.

MR. KATZ: That is too gloomy a picture, it seems to me. There are other findings to indicate that opinion in the United States is not crystallized in the direction of a warlike attitude toward Russia. For example, while many believe in the inevitability of conflict when the question is posed that way, you can still find a majority of the people, 55 per cent in fact, saying that they believe war can be prevented. Now, when you get contradictory findings such as these in opinion polling, it points very clearly toward uncrystallized opinion, because the weaker the beliefs, the more they are affected by angling the question from different approaches. Moreover, if you pursue the matter further, you will find that the American people as a whole have friendly feelings toward the Russian people as distinguished from Russian leaders. Nor do they see much cause for conflict in terms of economic issues. Mention was made a while back of our unwillingness to give up sovereignty, and yet 56 per cent of the people answered in the affirmative when they were asked whether they thought the United Nations should be strengthened, to make it a world government with power to control the armed forces of all the nations, including the United States. Thirty per cent were against it and ten per cent were undecided. Finally, I think the most important, hopeful finding concerns the various determinants of these opinions. Analysis shows that the people with more education, who know more about the problem, are much more hopeful of a solution, much more tolerant, much more ready to wait before taking drastic steps. For example, 10 per cent of the high-information group think war is certain, as against three times that many of the low-information group. In other words, to get back to that vicious circle, we do not have a compulsive force, if they really take account of public opinion, that would compel the leaders of this country to move in the direction of war.

MR. FESTINGER: Well, certainly the whole answer to the problem doesn't lie in getting information about American people and the pressures that they exert on their leaders. We also have to understand something about people in other countries and the pressures that they put on their leaders.

MR. CARTWRIGHT: Yes, I think that's right and I think we can learn something about public opinion in other countries. Public opinion polls are not confined exclusively to the United States. As a matter of fact, they exist in some 12 or 15 countries now, and we're beginning to get evidence of the thinking of people in various countries on common issues. For example, let's take this matter of belief in the inevitability of war. I have here evidence from the United States, Denmark, Canada, the Netherlands, France, Australia, Britain, and Norway. In virtually all of these countries we find that more people feel that war is inevitable in the next ten or fifteen years than feel that it is not. We are beginning now to have evidence by which we can compare one country with another on such matters. We are only beginning to do this, and the countries I've mentioned there represent a small fraction of the world, but it is something that social scientists can do.

MR. McGRANAHAN: Yes, but unfortunately one country is left out of that list — Russia: which is of course the critical country in our present situation, and it seems quite unlikely anything like a public opinion poll will be instituted there.

MR. MARQUIS: Well, is there anything you could do to get this kind of information about Russia, short of operating a Gallup poll in the country?

MR. McGRANAHAN: Well, not with anything like the certainty with which we can get it for this country. But I think we can improve our present techniques. Our knowledge of that country today derives largely from the impressions of single individuals who look at Russia. Each sees something different, according to his particular preconceptions and prejudices. It is like looking at a cloud — different people will see different things, and it's difficult from these separate impressions to compile any kind of systematic picture. Now, it is possible even with our meager facilities to improve our understanding of Russia, it seems to me. Mr. Likert in a recent address has suggested, for one thing, that diplomats might well be trained in methods of obtaining and assessing psychological intelligence. The problem is what aspects of Russian opinion one should look for. If Russians talk with Americans, we want to know who these Russians are, from what classes they come, and under what circumstances they are speaking. We want to know the answers to specific questions: Under what conditions would they compromise with us? How are they reacting to the problems associated with the atomic bomb? We don't know the answers to these questions, but they should be carefully investigated. We might somehow persuade people going to Russia to ask specific questions or at least to bring up specific issues in conversation with Russians and to remember what the Russians answered and in what ways. We can analyze, through content analysis, Russian radio broadcasts and newspapers, and find out what the climate is — *i.e.*, the atmosphere of opinions under which the Russians are living.

But in addition to getting at opinion, I think it's necessary to go even further back, because you can get your statistics from public opinion polls, and yet to understand them you have to view them in a broader context. The problem here concerns the Russian mentality. Is there such a thing? Is it different from the American mentality? That, of course, is a problem of great difficulty. But there are techniques which we can use here also, which will suggest answers and tell us whether we must understand the Russians by assuming that they are just like ourselves, or whether we've got to realize that they have a different perspective and that values which seem good to them do not seem so to us. We might carry out analyses of their ideals or their basic values as expressed in their literature, in their motion pictures, in their plays, or in their philosophies. Their history should be carefully examined to see whether there are certain consistent traits running through it. Are Russian Communists a novel phenomenon or are they similar in many ways to Czarist Russians? These are problems which I think should be carefully studied by whatever systematic techniques we can use, and if we can get some understanding, it might help in solving some of our problems of relations between countries. Suppose two men get in a quarrel about an open window. One man wants fresh air, and the other man wants to avoid a draft. Well, on that elemental level, they'll probably get into a fight. But if they understand what they really want, they may install a ventilating system which will both provide fresh air and avoid draft. Essentially, that's what America must do with Russia. We must find out what really the Russians want and what we want.

Dr. Miller: Mr. McGranahan, you have been telling us in this symposium about a technique you used in studying the plays of the German people, viewing them as a type of projective technique on a social level, with American plays as a sort of normal control. Would it be possible to use a method of that sort, do you think, in analyzing the present Russian national world view?

Mr. McGranahan: I see no reason why it couldn't be done. One problem would be that the Russian plays are censored and they're not really so much a free expression of fantasy as they are in this country. Yet, while there is a very rigorous political censorship, there are certain areas which are not censored. The relationships within a family presumably are not dictated by the Russian censors. If we could understand the Russian's psychological relations within his family, we might get some insight into his basic psychological traits which would help us to understand his relations to us.

Mr. Festinger: Of course, it might also be important for us to understand the Russian censor.

Dr. Miller: I have been wondering during this discussion whether it would not be possible to apply both to American statesmen and to the leaders of foreign countries some of the techniques of clinical psychology and psychiatry. We have developed methods for assessing personality which are becoming rapidly more precise, more effective, and more insightful. Efforts were made during the war to analyze all the data that were available about Hitler, for example, in order to understand his personality. Energies were devoted in that direction simply because it was recognized that the vicious circle that Mr. Marquis mentioned might exist, the people forcing their leaders to action and the leaders in turn taking action which they think reflects the attitude of the people, international aggression resulting. It was generally recognized that the leader was of paramount importance in this circle.

We might very well get all the material together that we have on Stalin and Molotov and the others of the Politbureau who determine so much of Russian foreign policy, and analyze their statements, not only objectively, but perhaps projectively. Also we could collect as much material as we can about their earlier lives in order to make a longitudinal analysis of the development of their personalities. Of course, such clinical studies are difficult even under the most satisfactory conditions when the subject of your study is in the same room with you. It is vastly more difficult when he is surrounded by the towers of the Kremlin, or even by the pillars of the State Department, and consequently protected from direct clinical observation.

MR. McGRANAHAN: I'm worried especially about the question of what practical action can be taken. Suppose we got all this knowledge and detailed information about public opinion in this country and Russia, our leaders and the Russian leaders, what can we do about it? Could we get people to act on it? Or would they simply use it as means of exploiting each other? It seems to me we have a basic problem as to the use of knowledge. Even though we haven't got it yet, we're still faced with the problem of how it would be used.

MR. LIPPITT: It does seem to me that this is a most important question. We've been thinking about what kind of information we can get and a little bit about what kind of information we do have. Now there is another aspect of the matter — changing the attitudes of the persons involved. On the one hand there is the average American, to take the person about whom we have the most information, who seems to be having considerable anxiety, whether it's open or behind the scenes of consciousness. And on the other hand there are the authorities. Don't we face the issue, then, of what we know, what techniques we have, for going about the problem of changing the attitudes that now exist? I'd like to suggest that we might break down the problem into three areas, if you will. One would be the changing of "grass-roots" public opinion: the whole matter of breaking the vicious circle at the level of public reaction. Another, aimed at a more strategic type of thinking, would be to change the attitudes of key people who exert the strongest influence on the international negotiators. The third would be to determine what kind of consulting relationship social scientists can work out which might be of some help in influencing directly the State Department officials, the American delegations to the United Nations, and so on. Does that supply a useful framework?

MR. FRENCH: Yes, indeed, but isn't one step missing? Don't we need to know more about the causes? That is, we need to know not only the state of public opinion, but what determines it before we can think most effectively about what to do about it. And I'd like to throw that question back to those of you who talked about that.

MR. KATZ: There's a lot of evidence to indicate that events as reported in the press have paramount importance in the determination of present-day attitudes toward Russia. For well-informed people, they have one effect. For the people who don't follow the news very carefully they have another effect. To the majority of the people, who don't read very critically, international events are pretty remote. They don't analyze or digest very carefully. But personalities are very important. The things that come into their immediate horizon are the personalities — the American representatives and the Russian representatives. The continual report of unpleasant personal incidents leaves an unfavorable residual effect, even though the American people wouldn't be able to analyze it carefully. Then one other great determinant of attitudes toward Russia is the factor mentioned earlier, attitudes toward the principles of communism, which Americans do not separate from Russia.

MR. CARTWRIGHT: It seems to me that another determinant is the sort of statements that are made in our media of mass communication about international affairs. What gets into the headlines about the function of the United Nations? Mainly ideas of conflict. What a person who runs and reads gets out of the press and over the radio today are the points of disagreement — the times when Russia walks out of a conference or when there is a veto or when somebody loses his temper, and so on. When something constructive is done, when an agreement is reached — these events do not receive emphasis.

MR. MARQUIS: Are you suggesting that we must censor our newspapers and the radio?

MR. CARTWRIGHT: No, I'm sure that would not be the conclusion. But I do think we might try to develop a feeling of social responsibility among the people who are in charge of these channels of communication, to think through a bit the significance of what they do upon the state of world opinion. It seems to me there are techniques we could employ for educating those people and demonstrating through research techniques the effect of their statements on world opinion. Something of that sort was done during the last war. Floyd Allport conducted a study of the effect of headlines concerning, for example, naval losses. His question was whether it was good or bad for morale to play up our losses instead of playing them down. There was objective research on the effects upon morale. It turned out that what was good for sales wasn't necessarily good for general morale. It seems to me that it is perfectly possible to make similar studies concerning international issues. Such research might well have a direct bearing on practices of our mass mediums which affect the development of opinion.

Mr. SZILARD: Perhaps, if we kept the headline from saying the opposite of the text, that would accomplish our purpose.

Mr. CARTWRIGHT: Well, I think studies have demonstrated objectively what the facts about the effects of distortion by press and radio are, and I think calling them to the attention of the public would be beneficial. I think we can educate the public in what it may expect from its media of communication as well as make the gatekeepers of these channels more sensitive to their responsibilities.

Dr. MILLER: I wonder if it wouldn't be possible, also, to make use of the fairly thorough knowledge that we now have of the psychology of advertising. We have learned how to influence large segments of the population to accept certain products, and to convince them of the value of eating certain foods. Cannot we rely on the fact stated earlier in the round table that there is basic good will and desire for peace among a large majority of the citizens of the world? Let us effect world action by pointing out that these techniques are available to them and can be used effectively to direct the thoughts and actions of others toward the goals that men of good will throughout the world do want.

Mr. McGRANAHAN: The difficulty there, it would seem to me, is that we don't know exactly yet what our goal should be with regard to solving the atomic bomb problem. If we had in detail a program of action which would succeed in solving the mess, and if it were a rational program, we could probably put it across quite easily by newspaper advertising and whatnot. But so far I haven't seen the rational proposal that would be convincing.

MR. SZILARD: Are the methods of advertising really applicable? Can you sell peace the way you sell toothpaste?

MR. FRENCH: I would answer no to that. I think we have a rather different kind of problem here. Let us suppose, for example, that we spend a great deal of money trying to do something about the atomic bomb through the mass media. Let's suppose we mobilize the newspapers, the radio, the magazines, and all those techniques.

MR. McGRANAHAN: In Russia as well as here?

MR. FRENCH: We're talking now about public opinion in this country, where we would have some opportunity to do that. I still think we would not be able to change public attitudes predictably even if we knew what we wanted, and what our values were. I think it is one thing to say, "Go and buy such and such a cosmetic" and another to convince the public to take specific international actions. Probably the best we can do through the mass media is to increase people's knowledge and information, and in this I hope we do an increasingly better job than we have.

MR. MARQUIS: Is there any other way to get at it? It's a rather naïve first suggestion to advocate putting on a radio campaign to sell the people peace and, as you say, it probably won't work. What other ways are there for the knowledge of the social sciences to be made useful, available, and influential?

DR. MILLER: Well, I wonder whether it wouldn't be possible to conduct crucial experiments to demonstrate in a quantitative fashion the point that certain types of headlines do form sentiments in certain directions and that the omission of other material which may not appear so newsworthy prevents healthy sentiments from being formed? When we have crucial experiments of that sort, which are clearly definitive, then we can present the facts to those who have control of the means of communication and say, "If you are men of good will, you will recognize that you have the control of public attitudes in your power and that such and such techniques, which we can indicate to you, will enable you to control those attitudes in one direction or the other."

MR. LIPPITT: I think we certainly can do a great deal of experimentation there. I would agree with Mr. French's implication, however, that results have not been too promising from the research that you've alluded to on getting changes in food-choice habits. Even in such minor matters, let's say, as eating kidney (which was one of the research programs we carried on during the war), not only did mass communication through the newspapers prove relatively ineffectual, but even good exhortatory lectures by nutrition experts with charts for housewives on how to buy kidney or escarole, and then how to cook it so the odor wouldn't permeate the house, and so on, did not produce marked results of the sort desired. On the other hand, when it was assumed that the individual is not the basic unit of action but when recognition was given to what Mr. Gibson referred to in his paper as social reinforcement of the learning situation through interaction in a group so that a discussion was held followed by a face-to-face commitment on the part of housewives that they would go out and buy some kidney, they were more likely to do so. Though these housewives never saw each other again, a very high percentage lived up to their commitment.

Following up this principle, I think you might be interested that we've had discussions with the physicist group in Cambridge on their problems of working with audiences for the purpose of frightening them into productive action. We have become very interested in this problem of what can be done with an audience group to make it possible for them to have an educational experience that will lead them to action on the problems raised by the atomic bomb, which is much different from hearing a lecture and going home to forget it completely. We started out this summer with one little field experiment in that direction in which Mr. French was deeply involved.

MR. FRENCH: We carried out what might be called a preliminary phase of field experimentation on the hypothesis that more powerful effects can be exerted in a face-to-face situation than in other sorts of relationships. With a group of about 75 intelligent laymen we put on an evening meeting lasting about two hours, in which we wanted to try out certain techniques of influencing the people to think, to get ready to act, and to plan for future actions after the meeting.

MR. LIPPITT: I should think it might be good to point out that as far as the program arrangers were concerned, there was no plan to put across to the audience any viewpoint. We are concerned only with methods for getting the group to do some thinking and for moving them from that thinking into whatever action it led to.

MR. FRENCH: That is, as social scientists we did not feel we could choose which organization concerned with atomic energy should be supported. As technicians, though, we thought we ought to be able to help any such organization put on a program that would get people to think more, to understand more, to do more about the issues facing them. The program roughly consisted of, first, a survey of the members of the audience to get an idea of what were their attitudes, how worried they were, and how much they thought about these matters. Then the meeting was held. Then there was a retest of attitudes after the meeting.

MR. LIPPITT: Before the meeting we asked them what they were then doing about the atomic problem and why they weren't doing more, and got a fine long list of rationalizations of various types for not doing anything.

MR. FRENCH: Also some statements of guilt feelings.

MR. LIPPITT: The meeting planners, in attempting to start out with a close relationship to the audience, took account of these statements. The proceedings began dramatically with a "Mr. Everyman," who had been in the audience, sitting on the stage reading a newspaper and throwing it down with disgust because of all the stuff about the atomic bomb, the international affairs stuff splattered all over the headlines. He threw down his newspaper and made some remark about his inability to do anything about it. Then he gave voice to the various rationalizations and guilt feelings of the audience and interacted with a "Super-ego" who spoke over a loud-speaker and who answered these rationalizations realistically, pointing them out to him for what they were and driving him into the corner of recognizing that he had responsibilities.

MR. FRENCH: I'd like to point out here that those techniques were effective, partly because we had used information from a survey. We knew what rationalizations the people had, and they heard their own words coming back at them from the stage.

MR. LIPPITT: Then the point for each member of the audience was: I'm Mr. Everyman. All right, I do feel I have some responsibility perhaps, but what are some of the facts about the situation? Well, he had noticed before he threw down his newspaper that the radio program included something on the atomic bomb that evening, so he switched on the radio. (We would have used a nuclear physicist if we had had one, but instead we had to use a radio and a recording in which basic data about the threat of the bomb were presented dramatically.) After that Mr. Everyman said, "All right, I'm scared. I've got responsibilities. So what? What can I do?" That's when you came on, as I recall, Mr. French.

MR. FRENCH: Yes. We developed the meeting from there on into panel groups, each of about six or eight persons, with representatives of different types of organizations. They came right up out of the audience to sit with us. This man did training in industry; that woman was a PTA leader; and so forth. The panels then discussed what they could do as individuals.

MR. LIPPITT: And also as group members, members of organizations, social leaders.

MR. FRENCH: As group members. Isolated individuals may not be able to function effectively without support, but they can when they have connections with a group. Well, to make a long story short, the panels discovered enough that could be done by many organizations so that it was decided that it would be a good thing to set up a research and information institute — an Office of Atomic Information — which would do two things: first, conduct research on how to help such groups as these people represented in their actions on international affairs; and second, supply them with information available on international events. Now, as a final test of the effectiveness of this method of communication, we said at the end of the meeting, "All right now, suppose we're setting this institute up. We would like to get pledges from those people who are interested in supporting it, either by spending some time on it or by pledging money. We handed out slips, and from a small and probably not-too-wealthy audience, a sum of something like $370 was pledged.

MR. MARQUIS: We should have done that tonight.

MR. LIPPITT: What they came to see was that an organization of consultants was needed to help with the question of how people in general can be motivated to take responsibility for international affairs. That was what they pledged money for.

MR. FRENCH: Now, I'd like to suggest what might be possible next research steps along this line, just to complete the picture. I think it would be feasible to set up a whole series of such experiments, conducted perhaps by many universities and many social psychologists all over the country, and to have field surveys which would measure the effectiveness of these methods. In that way we could employ a nice combination of our techniques, both for measuring and assessing attitudes and for producing changes in public opinion.

MR. LIPPITT: In fact, we have worked out a design for research as a result of this little experiment. In a given community we would carry through a survey of the type that Mr. Katz and Mr. Cartwright have described. Then we would hold two types of meetings in that community, each with a similar group of community leaders. In one we would use the exhortation technique; in the other, our "group-thinking" technique just described. We would then follow the changes of attitudes and actions of these leaders which resulted from the two different types of approach. In this way we could learn the best methods of motivating them to action.

MR. MCGRANAHAN: It seems to me that that kind of research, however, must be secondary to a more fundamental kind of research which will provide information to people as to what they might do. I don't see much point in getting people aroused with a feeling of responsibility to do something, unless we can provide information to help them decide on a course of action.

MR. LIPPITT: On the basis of our experience I wouldn't agree with you at all. People can do a remarkable job of finding out what to do if they are helped to get hold of the information they need to think out the problem. That's what we saw in our experiment. The participants in it developed excellent group and individual practical programs. They worked out their channels of influence and communication; for example, between the PTA and a woman on a United Nations commission. Such plans developed rapidly as soon as they got going on them.

MR. MARQUIS: I'm going to terminate our discussion now with a statement of our hope that, even though we are in the humblest beginning stages of social psychology, nevertheless it has been made apparent that its findings can be usefully applied to the pressing issues before the world today.

INDEX

A

Absenteeism, 72
Action research, 14
Advertising, 188, 189
Aesthetics, 5
Aggression and leadership, 35
  and organization, 36
Alger, Horatio, 136
Allport, F., 187
Allport, G. W., 152*n*., 154*n*., 157,
  160–162
"Alone-and-together" experiments,
  81
Altruism, 165
American films (*see* Films)
American-German national
  differences, 99*ff*.
Animal behavior versus human
  behavior, 153
Anonymity (*see* Voting)
Anthropology, 15, 21, 96, 158
  anthropometric, 9
  cultural, 94, 151
  social, 10, 15
Anticipation (*see* Reward)
Area sampling, 67
Area study, 15
Astronomy, 4, 13
Atom bomb, advertising a rational
  program for, 188
  American attitudes toward, 177
  versus British attitudes, 172

Atom bomb, American attitudes
  toward public opinion polls,
  176, 179
  field experiment in, 190–193
  flying saucers and, 178
  London Conference and, 173
  Potsdam Conference and, 174
  psychological aspects of,
    174, 175
  Russia and, 173, 180, 181
  social psychology and,
    171–178*ff*.
Attitudes and habits, hierarchy of,
  161
  patterns of, 20
Authoritarian atmosphere, 83
  and group process, 19
Authoritarian and laissez-faire
  leadership, 22, 34
Authoritarian supervision, 76

B

Bacon, 8
Bavelas, Alex, 84
Benét, Stephen V., *The Devil and
  Daniel Webster*, 141
Bible, 172
Biologic drives (*see* Drives)
Biology, 4
Boston area, 38
Botany, 6, 9
Bradford, 91*n*.